Teaching About Energy

Practical Activities for 7-11 year olds

Contents

The Centre for Alternative Technology (C.A.T.)

This book has been published in association with the Centre for Alternative Technology. The Centre for Alternative Technology is a visitor centre which is used by thousands of school and college students every year.

School visits

At C.A.T. visitors can see in action an impressive collection of windmills, water power, solar water heating, solar electricity, energy conservation, energy efficient buildings and organic growing.

They travel on the water-powered cliff railway which carries visitors up to the site all summer long. They can touch windmills, see a water turbine turning, feel hot water from solar panels, make waves to generate power, and take home with them ideas on how to save energy in their own homes and schools and how to make compost and grow organically in their own gardens.

The Education Officers provide educational services for school and college students on day visits and residential courses at every level, including infants, special schools, A-level science, Geography and Technology, and teacher training.

Inset

The Education Officers provide in-service and teacher training and consultancy.

Eco-cabins

When they stay in the residential 'Eco-cabins' pupils monitor and control their own energy system (using wind, water and solar power), enjoying a unique and stimulating residential experience. Courses are tailor made to the needs of the group.

Public Courses

C.A.T. runs public courses for individuals on a range of topics (including courses for teachers), produces publications for pupils, teachers and the general public and has a mail order service for C.A.T. publications and kits, as well as a variety of other resources.

Contact:

Education Officer, C.A.T., Machynlleth, Powys, SY20 9AZ

Tel: 01654 703743 Fax: 01654 703605

Website: www.cat.org.uk

e-mail: cat@catinfo.demon.co.uk

mailorder@catmailorder.demon.co.uk

Copyright © Clare Eastland
Copyright © Illustrations: Chris Wakefield

First published 1999 by Southgate Publishers Ltd in association with The Centre for Alternative Technology
Southgate Publishers Ltd 15 Barnfield Avenue, Exmouth, Devon EX8 2QE

Printed and bound in Great Britain by Short Run Press, Exeter, Devon.

This book has been printed on ecology offset recycled/chlorine free paper.

British Library Cataloguing in Publication Data.
A CIP catalogue record for this book is available from the British Library.

ISBN 1-85741-088-2

Chapter 1 Introduction

This book has been written to provide teachers with a range of interesting activities to help them to teach about energy at Key Stage 2 with an emphasis on sustainability and alternative technologies.

Energy is the foundation on which industries and our whole economy is built. In recent years there have been threats to our environment from traditional uses of energy and a new emphasis on sustainability. These issues are important to our pupils, and dealt with in geography, but are rarely reflected in teaching materials for science and design and technology.

The activities in this book are intended to be interesting and fun for pupils. Many have practical relevance and involve the use of inexpensive junk or scrap materials. They are designed to meet National Curriculum requirements for areas of Science, Geography and Design and Technology in particular. A great deal of basic science and technology can be taught through these activities, especially in the areas of energy, materials and their properties, physical processes, weather, heat, and light. There are many opportunities for design and make challenges. There are also links specified with other curriculum areas such as history, English and mathematics. There is a section showing the specific links with the National Curriculum at the end of the book (see page 61).

There are five chapters each dealing with a particular source of energy: the sun, plants, animals, wind, and water, followed by a chapter on storing and conserving energy. Within each chapter the order of the activities is designed to take teacher and pupils logically through the concepts, beginning with understanding where the energy comes from and how we can observe and measure it, through to how it can be used in simple ways. Teachers should choose those activities they think are right for their pupils. Some activities extend work from others earlier in the same chapter.

The activities provided are all suitable for use at Key Stage 2 (KS2), although they vary in difficulty of concepts and in the level of practical skills they require. They include investigations, experiments, games, design and make projects, and demonstrations. Some are simple enough for individual work, others best done by children working in small groups, and some may be better made and demonstrated by the teacher in whole class teaching. Some things to be made are working models, others have some real practical use. Detailed suggestions and clear diagrams are provided, and the activities are intended to be introduced with a problem solving approach, asking questions such as 'What do you think would happen if.....?' or 'How could we find out......?' or 'How could we devise a fair test for......?

At the end there is a small section of photocopiable sheets for pupils to work on in class or take home, and a list of useful organisations/suppliers and resources.

Safety

All the activities in this book should be undertaken with common sense safety precautions and adult supervision, and following school guidance. A few should be undertaken with particular care and these are indicated with a safety symbol.

Key Concepts

In each chapter background information of use to non-specialist teachers is provided in tinted boxes. Some of the key concepts which the book is intended to help teachers get across, are listed below.

 1. All energy comes from the sun.

This is broadly true, with the exception of tidal and nuclear energy. Tidal energy is caused by the moon's movements, which are only indirectly caused by the sun. Nuclear energy is outside the scope of this book, but is produced by splitting a heavy atomic nucleus such as uranium.

In each chapter there is information and activities on how the particular energy source (e.g. water power) gets its energy from the sun.

 2. Energy flows along food chains.

Work is provided on this, especially in chapters 3 and 4.

 3. Energy sources are of different types. The main distinction is between renewable and non-renewable energy.

Renewable energy includes solar, water, wind energy, and also plant energy and animal energy. Renewable energy sources need not run out. Generally they are cleaner than fossil fuels.

Non-renewable energy sources are fossil fuels such as oil, coal and gas. Although we cannot know exactly how much of these resources are left on Earth as more are still being discovered, these sources are being used up too quickly. They are also more polluting than renewable sources.

Some activities involve comparing energy from different sources.

 4. Use of all sources of energy has an impact on the environment.

We cannot survive without using some energy resources. Therefore we need to work on how we can reduce this impact by using renewable energy sources in appropriate ways and conserving energy.

Many activities, especially in the final chapter, but also elsewhere, ask pupils to look at how they use energy and how they can conserve it.

Chapter 2 Energy from the Sun

The sun

The sun is the source of our energy or power, either directly or indirectly. The sun's energy millions of years ago enabled photosynthesis by plants, the remains of which we use in the form of fossil fuels - oil, coal and gas (see chapter 3, page 23). Energy is released when fuels are burnt. The sun's energy today is responsible for winds and waves, and for the rainfall which enables running water to be used for hydro-electric power. The sun's energy is used by plants to produce food and so plant fuels such as wood. Animals get their energy by eating plants or other animals. Plant, animal, water and wind power will be dealt with in later chapters, but this chapter will suggest activities for teaching about the direct power of the sun.

The school and its grounds provide many opportunities for children to investigate and explore the sun's energy. In the following pages activities are grouped by topic. The aim is to give pupils an appreciation of the importance of the sun, to understand how we can harness the sun's energy directly as a clean, safe and renewable form of energy.

The sun in the solar system

One starting point for learning about the energy of the sun might be through work on the planets and the solar system. If pupils are familiar with scale from map work, then you might like to try to make a map of the solar system in the school playground. You could do this with pupils representing the planets, rather than drawing them on the ground, at least initially. The activity of deciding on a suitable scale and trying to work out the distances will in itself impress on pupils the huge distances involved.

Be careful to warn children not to look directly at the sun.

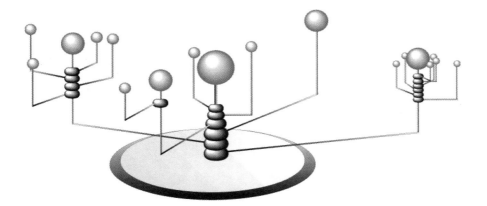

Getting the sizes of planets in scale as well as the distances can be quite a problem. If you were to make circular cut-outs of the planets and sun to lay down on the playground on the same scale as below, then the sun would be only 1.4 cm in diameter and all the planets would be much smaller. Ask the children for their suggestions. The only sensible alternative if you want to show both distances from the sun and the sizes of the heavenly bodies in one go, is to increase the diameters of the sun and planets to one hundred times what they should be on the scale below. You may decide this is too difficult for your children, but if you want to have a go the sizes (diameters) would be: Sun 140cm, Mercury 5mm, Pluto 6mm, Mars 7mm, Venus 1.2cm, Earth 1.3cm, Neptune 5cm, Uranus 5.2cm, Saturn 12cm, Jupiter 14.3cm.

Fig 2. The solar system

The pictures below show the relative sizes of the sun and planets at 1/2,000,000,000 scale. Even at this scale the distance from the Sun to Pluto is 6 kilometres.
Also, on the playground scale suggested right, the moon should stand only 3.8mm from the Earth. On the same scale the next nearest stars after the sun should all be well over 400km away.

Planets in solar system with average distances from the sun, and suggested playground scale		
Details:	Average distance from the sun	Playground scale
Mercury	60,000,000 km	60 cm
Venus	110,000,000 km	1 m 10 cm
Earth	150,000,000 km	1 m 50 cm
Mars	230,000,000 km	2 m 30 cm
Jupiter	780,000,000 km	7 m 80 cm
Saturn	1,430,000,000 km	14m 30 cm
Uranus	2,870,000,000 km	28m 70 cm
Neptune	4,500,000,000 km	45m exactly
Pluto	5,910,000,000 km	59m 10 cm

NB Rounded off to nearest 10,000,000 km. This allows playground version to be given to nearest 10 cm. Average distances of planets from the sun are used because no orbit is totally circular and some can vary a lot.

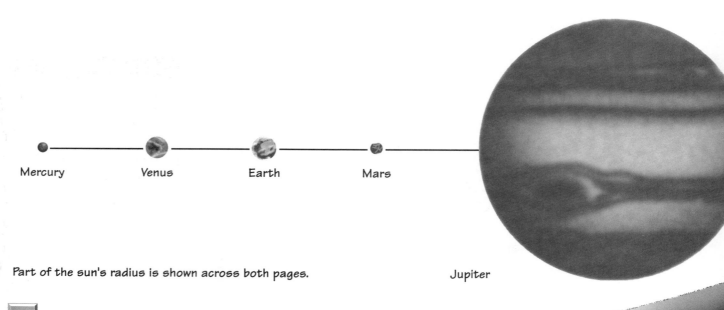

Mercury   Venus   Earth   Mars

Jupiter

Part of the sun's radius is shown across both pages.

Sun and Shadows

Shadow clock

Make a simple shadow clock using a metre of dowelling. Stand the dowelling upright in the cut-off bottom of a washing-up liquid container, filled with wet sand. Stand the clock on a level surface, preferably concrete, away from buildings or other shadows. At every hour exactly, draw in the shadow cast by the clock using chalk. Pupils can measure the length of the shadows and compare them, and the angles between the shadow lines. Try making a shadow clock early in the year, perhaps in the spring term, using a more permanent marker and then another later, in the summer term. Is there any difference in the shadows cast? (A shadow stick is available from Technology Teaching Systems.)

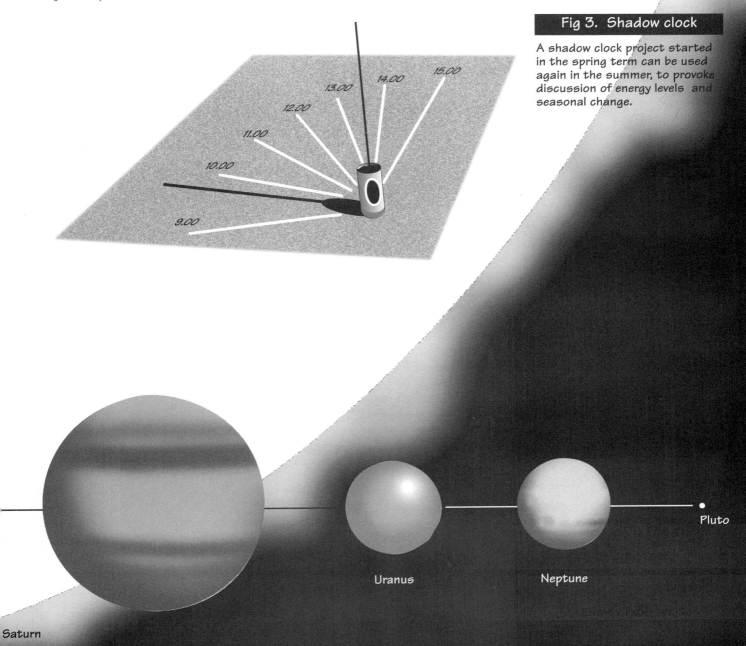

Fig 3. Shadow clock

A shadow clock project started in the spring term can be used again in the summer, to provoke discussion of energy levels and seasonal change.

9.00
10.00
11.00
12.00
13.00
14.00
15.00

Saturn

Uranus

Neptune

Pluto

Measuring shadows

Ask pupils to measure the shadows of buildings, trees, other objects and themselves at different times of the day. Can they explain why the shadows are not always the same length? Can they explain why they change direction through the day? Get them to relate the shadows' direction to cardinal points and the movement of the sun in the sky. You could mark not only a compass rose on the school playground, but also pictures to indicate the directions of sun rise and sunset, and perhaps an arrowed line to indicate the direction of the sun's movement overhead.

Sundials

Could you install a sundial in the playground? You could buy one, or alternatively mark one on the playground, following the same principles as for the shadow clock above, but so that the shadow-stick is formed by a person standing on a square or point. Also see **'Make a Sundial'**, published by the British Sundial Society and available from Technology Teaching Systems.

Fig 4. Landscape sundial with the observer as the gnomon

Observing cloud cover

Take pupils outside so that they can see as much of the sky as possible. Ask them to estimate the amount of cloud cover as a proportion or percentage of the whole sky they can see. Younger pupils may find it easier to draw clouds onto a circular piece of paper or paper plate, and colour them in. They can then estimate how much of the paper is covered. To avoid cricked necks you could begin by looking down at part of the sky seen in a mirror. Once pupils have become fairly proficient at estimating they could keep records by estimating at the same time each day for a week or month. Design a system for recording the cloud cover or use the conventional system of sectors in a circle. Compare your findings with temperatures for the same period - is it always hotter when there is less cloud?

Sunshine plan of school grounds

Another way in to work on the sun's power might be to draw a plan of the school grounds with the positions of sunrise and sunset and movements of the sun marked on it, along with the sunniest and shadiest spots. Start by photocopying or drawing an ordinary plan and including anything big enough to cast a shadow in the grounds. Discuss which are the sunniest and shadiest spots at different times.

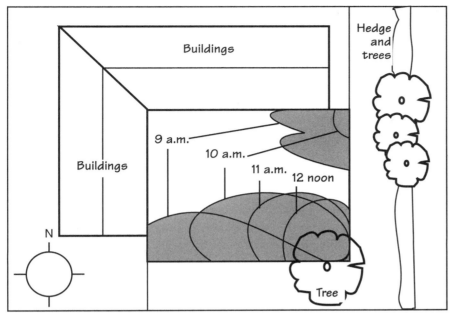

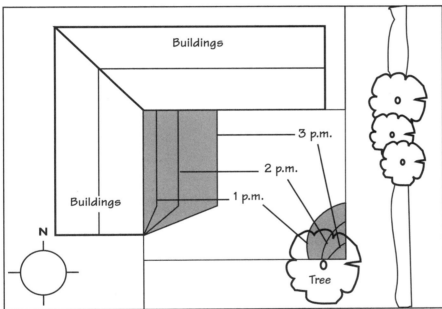

Fig 5. Sunshine plans

Select a suitable study area in the school grounds for this work.

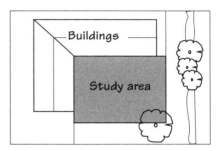

A morning solar plan with chalk lines (shown black here) drawn around the edge of the shadows on the playground at hourly intervals.

An afternoon solar plan with chalk lines drawn using the same method as the morning session.

Discuss the effects of shelter and wind on the temperature in different places. The children could use thermometers to test for the hottest spots, but will these necessarily be the sunniest places in terms of hours of sunshine? You could even produce a class map (similar to temperature maps) showing lines linking places with the same amount of full sunshine in a day. Or a simpler alternative using coloured squares on squared paper. (A solar observatory kit for recording the movements of the sun is available from Commotion.)

Look at the differences between light and shade in the playground. Compare intense shade from buildings, dappled shade from beneath tree canopies, shade produced by moving cloud cover and intensity of light and shade at different times of day. This can be done by observation, measurement using a long tape measure, or measurement using an old-fashioned photographic light-metre, separate from a camera. It is easiest to use a clean plan each time you go out to record. At the end of the day you can work out how many hours of sunlight you get in each area. The results can be displayed in graphs or on a map of the playground, perhaps using an IT graphics package. You can adapt the light and shade record sheet on page 19 to suit your own situation.

Sun drying

Show the power of the sun by using it for drying. On a breezy day most of the drying power outside comes from the wind, but on a hot, still summer's day it is possible to dry wet clothes. Discuss why using a clothes line is better than using a tumble-drier. Experiment to see what the best angle is for drying - flat on the ground, at 45 degrees, or at 90 degrees? Food is often sun-dried in tropical countries so this could be related to your 'other locality' study in geography. You could even try drying tomatoes or chillies in the sun here.

Flowers such as lavender or statice can be grown and dried for winter flower displays, though in strong sunlight they will fade. You could also watch how the sun dries flower and grass seeds, so assisting in spreading the seeds and plant reproduction. To eliminate wind from your sun-drying experiments place things behind plastic or glass, but make sure they are ventilated. The plastic prevents heat from escaping so quickly. Go on from these experiments to design a solar dryer. In real life, of course you would want to use the power of the wind in drying too, so a good dryer may be open.

Fig 6. A solar dryer

An air flow is established which removes moisture from the object being dried.

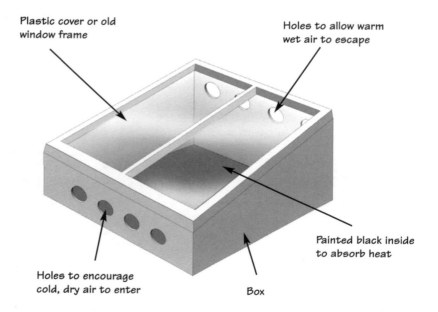

Plastic cover or old window frame

Holes to allow warm wet air to escape

Painted black inside to absorb heat

Holes to encourage cold, dry air to enter

Box

Evaporation

A simple experiment to show the sun's power in evaporating water is to place two jars of water on a sunny window sill. Put the same amount of water in each and mark the level on the outside. Leave one uncovered. Watch to see how long it takes for all the water to evaporate. Cover the other jar tightly with a plastic bag. Watch to see what happens to the water level. Notice the little droplets of water on the inside of the bag as the water evaporates and then condenses again on the inside of the bag. Can the pupils explain where the water in the first jar has gone? Can they explain what happens to the water in the second jar? What happens if the two jars are placed somewhere cool out of the sun?

Heat-storing greenhouse

All greenhouses collect the sun's energy, but most lose it again fairly quickly. Design and build a greenhouse which collects the sun's energy more effectively. Children can look at the shape and where the sun is, and think about how the sun is travelling through the sky. Build an insulated greenhouse to hold or store the sun's energy once it has been collected. Materials which insulate, such as polystyrene, bounce the heat off back into the greenhouse. Materials which store heat, such as cans of water, have a reasonable mass.

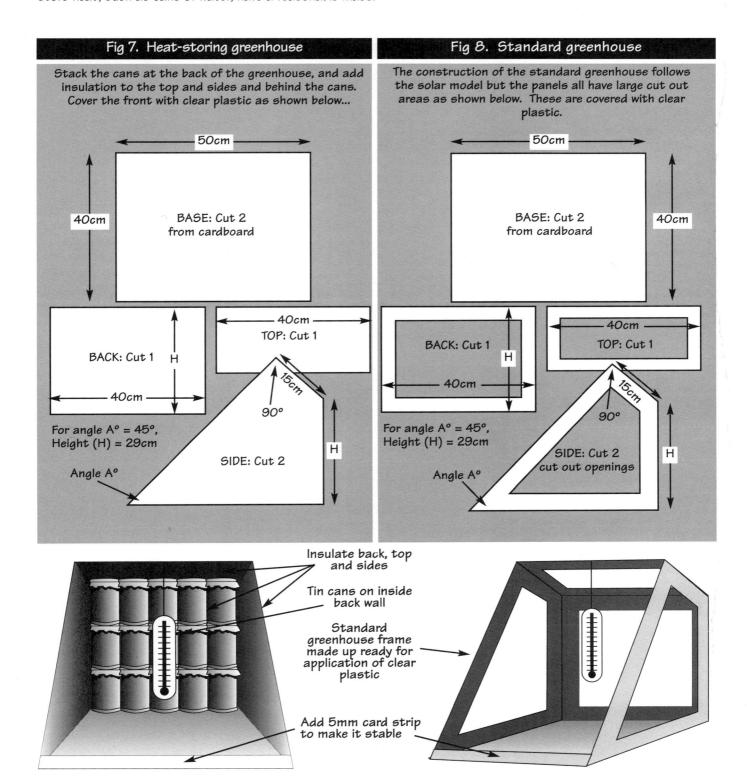

Fig 7. Heat-storing greenhouse

Stack the cans at the back of the greenhouse, and add insulation to the top and sides and behind the cans. Cover the front with clear plastic as shown below...

50cm

40cm

BASE: Cut 2 from cardboard

40cm
TOP: Cut 1

BACK: Cut 1   H

40cm

15cm

90°

SIDE: Cut 2   H

For angle A° = 45°, Height (H) = 29cm

Angle A°

Fig 8. Standard greenhouse

The construction of the standard greenhouse follows the solar model but the panels all have large cut out areas as shown below. These are covered with clear plastic.

50cm

40cm

BASE: Cut 2 from cardboard

40cm
TOP: Cut 1

BACK: Cut 1   H

40cm

15cm

90°

SIDE: Cut 2 cut out openings   H

For angle A° = 45°, Height (H) = 29cm

Angle A°

Insulate back, top and sides

Tin cans on inside back wall

Standard greenhouse frame made up ready for application of clear plastic

Add 5mm card strip to make it stable

Calculate the angle of the front panel to the sun (angle A°) by your geographical position. Your latitude plus 15°.

Face your solar greenhouse directly into the sun. Put a thermometer inside it and measure the temperature at intervals during the day. You could even put in a maximum and minimum thermometer to record the lowest temperature inside it at night. Screen the bulb of the thermometer from direct sunlight to be sure of measuring the air temperature.

You could also make an ordinary greenhouse, the same shape, but without the solar energy storing or insulating elements. (see diagram on page 11).

Compare the effectiveness of the two greenhouses.

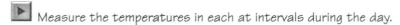 Measure the temperatures in each at intervals during the day.

Measure the minimum temperatures in each at night.

 After they have both reached a high temperature (perhaps at 2p.m. on a sunny day), put them both in the shade and measure the temperatures as they cool.

Try growing plants in both greenhouses and compare the results. Make sure you apply the same amounts of water and other conditions to both.

The results can be presented in graphs or pictograms using suns or tin-cans.

You could also try the following experiments:

changing the angle of the front panel to the sun;

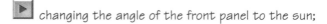 adding more insulating material, e.g. expanded polystyrene;

 using sand, soil or crumpled up newspaper instead of water in the tin cans, or leaving them empty.

Ask pupils to design and make their own insulated greenhouse using a variety of junk materials. They could make it big enough to grow seedlings in. They may find it useful to look at small commercially made plant propagators available in nurseries or garden centres, and to experiment further with solar collecting and insulating materials. (See also page 13.)

Collecting solar energy

Collect different small and large-sized aluminium pie-plates or aluminium containers from ready meals. You will need at least two: one which is wide and shallow, and one which is smaller and deeper. When they are empty, clean and dry, paint them black inside to make solar collectors. Use a non-water-soluble black paint. Add 100cc of water to each container. Then wrap cling-film around them and tape it in place. Place each solar collector on top of a stack of newspapers in the sun for 10 minutes. Then pour the water from each into a cup and measure the temperature. Which solar collector works best? Ask the pupils to suggest why the newspapers are necessary, and why the best solar collector is best, i.e. why it heats the same amount of water to a higher temperature.

Safety warning: expanded polystyrene can get too hot in strong sunlight and give off fumes.

Fig 9. Solar collectors

Aluminium containers are easily available in a variety of shapes and sizes. Painted black on the insides with water resistant paint, these make ideal solar collectors for a variety of experiments (see text).

(The best collector will be the widest and shallowest as it will collect more solar energy over a greater area to heat the same amount of water.)

Extend this by putting 100cc of water into a pan. Or use a solar collector of the 'best' kind. Start with it cool. Hold the container over a candle, using tongs. Heat the water to the same temperature you got using the best solar collector. (A candle is used here because it is safe and convenient, not because it is an alternative fuel.) Then talk about questions such as:

▶ Is this a fair test to compare solar and candle power?

▶ How long did it take to heat the water by each method?

▶ Is solar energy free?

▶ How much did the candle energy cost?

▶ How much energy was used to make the candle? Are all candles the same? Compare a beeswax candle, made locally, with a factory-made candle.

▶ What are the advantages of each kind of energy?

This would be a good lead in to work on domestic hot water heating. Ask children how their hot water is heated at home and what fuel is used. Make sure children understand what a fuel is.

Safety warning: take care when holding container over candle.

Using colours to absorb and reflect the sun's energy

Try a simple experiment to see which colours absorb the sun's heat best. Use pieces of different coloured heavy paper: white, black, blue, green and red. They should all be the same size. Place each piece of paper in the sun at the same time, in the same intensity of sunshine. One group of children could be responsible for each piece. Then place one ice cube in the middle of each piece of paper. The ice cubes should be all the same size and shape and placed on the paper at the same time. Ask pupils to predict beforehand which ice cube will melt first. Then use a timer to measure how quickly they melt. Go on to relate this evidence to the real world. What colour clothes are warmest and coolest? Should we change the colour of our cars in summer and winter?

Using different materials to absorb or reflect the sun's energy

Try the same experiment as above, using ice cubes, but instead of pieces of coloured paper, try using different kinds of materials. It is best to use materials of the same colour for a fair test. You could try comparing paper, wood, shiny metal (aluminium foil), dull metal, plastic and different kinds of fabric. Talk about the effects of the surfaces of the material - do shiny things absorb or reflect energy? Do things with a rough surface absorb more energy? Why might this be so? Relate this to the real world and to design possibilities. For example, what material should sun-hats be made of? What material should winter hats be made of?

Solar cooking

It is not difficult to cook food using solar energy, but it is important to use foods which can safely be eaten cold or uncooked, as it is much more fun if children can test the results by eating the food. The main problem with some solar cookers is that they have to be looked after and moved to ensure that the device collecting the solar energy is always in the best position to collect the most heat from the sun.

A solar oven

You can make a solar oven using a wooden or cardboard box with a piece of glass, plastic or clingfilm over the front, an insulated back and sides and a collector made of the box flaps covered in foil. This does have to be moved, and works best if the glass faces the sun. Suitable insulation might be polystyrene tiles, or beads kept in place with more card, or polystyrene packing from electrical goods.

Compare your oven with a cooking pot simply placed in the sun on its own and another placed in a black plastic bag in the sun. All three need to be in places with the same amount of sunshine, and to contain the same amount and type of food.

Apple baking

Ask children to test designs for an apple baker to bake slices of apple. The apple-baker is simply a solar oven which is not completely covered. For each apple baker you will need two plastic cups and a white paper cone. You will also need plastic food wrapping, aluminium foil, black paper or paint and newspaper or some other insulating material. Line the inside of a paper cup with black paper or paint it black inside, using non-toxic paint. Place an apple slice inside the cup and cover it with plastic food wrap. Make a large paper cone and wrap it around the cup. Place cone and cup inside another cup to hold everything together. Then add insulating material around the bottom of the cup, and stand it in full sun, aiming the cone at the sun. This can be done by propping the cone up at an angle. This is the basic or control model, using a white paper cone or solar collector. Compare this with collectors made by glueing aluminium foil to the inside of the cone. Children may like to try out other kinds or surfaces of collectors and different kinds of insulators.

Parabola cooker

Make a cooker for marshmallows, banana or apple slices or other 'kebabs'. (Note: marshmallows contain gelatin which comes from cattle.). You will need a long narrow box - the longer the better as this is where the heat is collected. A good size for the box is about 400mm long by 300mm wide. If you have an enlarging copier, photocopy the parabola template on page 18 at 141% (A4 to A3).

photocopy the parabola template on page 18 at 141% (A4 to A3).

Fig 10. A solar oven

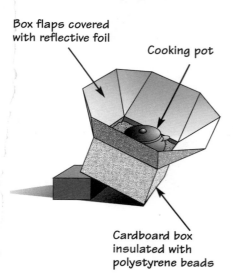

Box flaps covered with reflective foil

Cooking pot

Cardboard box insulated with polystyrene beads

Safety warning: expanded polystyrene can get too hot in strong sunlight and give off fumes.

Safety warning: use only foods which can be eaten uncooked or cold.

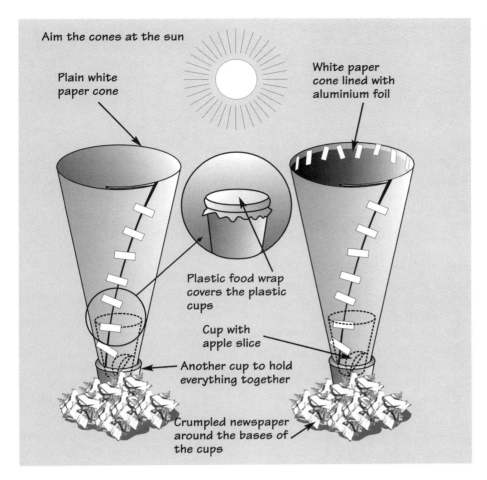

Aim the cones at the sun

Plain white paper cone

White paper cone lined with aluminium foil

Plastic food wrap covers the plastic cups

Cup with apple slice

Another cup to hold everything together

Crumpled newspaper around the bases of the cups

Fig 11. A solar apple baker

Compare different methods of cooking an apple slice by direct solar energy. One cooker uses a plain white paper cone reflector. The other uses an aluminium foil lined cone. The cones must be aimed towards the sun and crumpled newspaper around the base reduces heat loss during cooking.

Fig 12. Parabola cooker

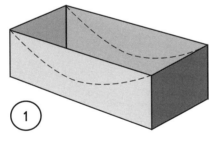

(1)

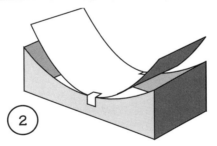

(2)

(3)

1. Use the template on page 18 to make a card template. Use this to trace the curve on the sides of the box. Make sure that it is centred and straight.

2. Use a knife or sharp scissors to cut out the curve very carefully. Measure and cut a piece of flexible cardboard to fit over the curved opening of the box.

3. Attach the cardboard to the box with tape. Begin at the centre, working outwards. Then glue aluminium foil to the surface of the curve. The foil needs to be as smooth as possible.

4. Cut two pieces of stiff cardboard to make supports at the sides of the curve. These will hold the spit for your food. Check the focal length from the curve up the side of the supports. Mark this point with a pen and make a hole each side. Use a metal skewer for the spit and thread your food onto it. Place the cooker in the sun and see how long it takes to cook. You may have to move your cooker to follow the sun.

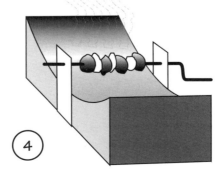

(4)

Try covering your parabola cooker with plastic to hold in the heat, or putting it in a polystyrene box. (Often these can be obtained from fruit and vegetable or electrical shops.) Sometimes these boxes have lids. If you cut a hole in the lid to allow the sun in and cover the hole with clear plastic you can make a parabola cooker in a box with a removable lid.

Passive solar heating

Passive solar heating means making it easy for solar energy to get into our buildings to heat them up. In Britain buildings get an average of 14% of their heating in this way, mostly from south-facing windows.

On a sunny day at midday or early afternoon, predict and then measure the temperatures in the following places and compare them:

▶ inside near a sunny south-facing window;

▶ inside near a north-facing window;

▶ inside in a cool shady place such as a corridor;

▶ outside in the sun;

▶ outside in the shade.

Talk about the reasons for the differences. Children may have noticed how much warmer it is near a south-facing window on a hot day. This can be true even in the winter. Talk about where this heat comes from. The glass allows the sun's rays to come through but then slows down the rate at which the heat escapes. Talk about double-glazing and insulated walls. Discuss with the children how their houses are heated. What fuel is used? Challenge them to design a house which collects the sun's rays or solar energy during the day and stores it so that it stays warm at night. How would they stop it getting too hot? Brainstorm ideas as a class or in groups. Then let children draw their designs.

Hot water heater

Make a simple hot water heater using flexible black tubing, a box, a piece of glass, plastic or clingfilm, two buckets and a clothes peg. Bicycle inner tubes are good for this as they are flexible and the rubber is thin, so the heat is transferred to the water quite quickly. Discuss the design of the heater with the children.

Test it out. Put the solar collector in a sunny place on a table or stand so that one bucket is below and one at the side. Fill the tube completely with water to form a siphon. Leave one end in the top bucket. Put your thumb over the other end to trap the water inside and, keeping your thumb in place, move that end of the tube into the lower bucket. Fit a peg to stop water loss then arrange the tubing in the heater box and cover it with plastic or clingfilm. Alternatively you can fill the tubing and the top bucket by connecting the lower end of the hose to the tap. When the top bucket is full, disconnect the tap and clamp the open end of the hose with a clothes peg until you are ready to start releasing the water through the heater. Once the water starts to flow use the peg to keep the water flow to a small trickle. This will enable the water to heat up. After a while the water trickling into the second bucket will be warmer than the water in the first bucket. Discuss how you can measure the temperatures and then do so. Try

2. Line the insides of the box with reflective foil.

3. Paint the inside base of the box matt black to warm the air in the box.

Fig 13. Solar hot water heater

1. Shallow cardboard or wooden box with insulated sides and base, or polystyrene broccoli box.

4. Loop the tubing backwards and forwards inside the box. Place the tubes as close together as possible covering the base.

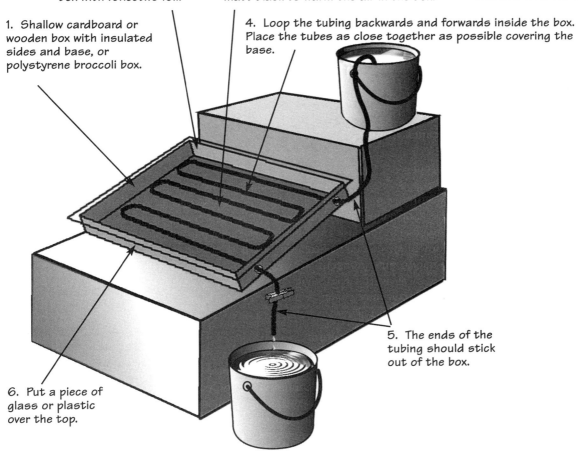

5. The ends of the tubing should stick out of the box.

6. Put a piece of glass or plastic over the top.

other types and colours of tubing for comparisons. Let the children suggest improvements to slow the heat escaping.

Discuss with children : How does the school heat its water? How do pupils' homes heat water? What fuels are used?

Using photovoltaic cells

Today many children and adults have solar-powered calculators and watches. These use photovoltaic cells, also called solar cells, which generate electricity when light falls on them. These cells are very thin and usually made from silicon. Although they are improving in efficiency they each produce only small amounts of electricity. Often they are used with a battery, so that the cells charge the battery during the day and the electricity is used whenever needed.

Brainstorm with the children the possible uses for photovoltaic cells. Solar kits, photovoltaic cells and motors are available from C.A.T. (see the Resources section). You can use these to compare the function of solar cells with other forms of energy, for example:

▶ compare the length of use of batteries and solar cells in watches and calculators and the comparative costs.

▶ make a small lightweight boat. Compare the power sources of wind (sail), battery and solar cell.

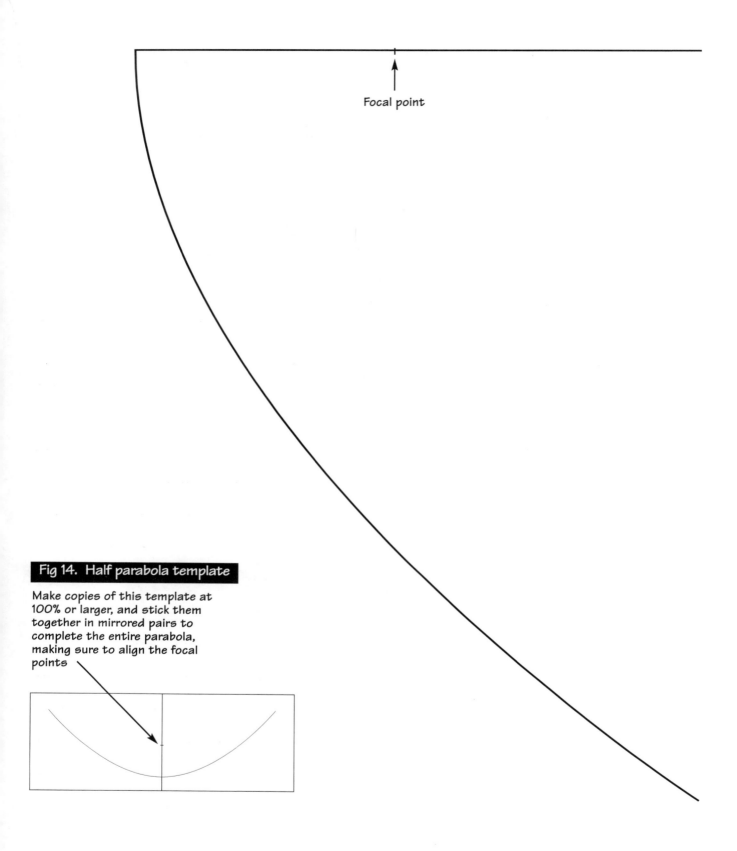

Focal point

Fig 14. Half parabola template

Make copies of this template at
100% or larger, and stick them
together in mirrored pairs to
complete the entire parabola,
making sure to align the focal
points

Light and shade record sheet

Fill in the temperature measurements below, along with your light and shade observations for each station on the school grounds map.

Date:... **Time:**..

Map station number	Temperature (°C)	Observation
		Light or shade, (strong shade, dappled shade, cloud cover, strong sunlight.)
1		
2		
3		
4		
5		
6		
7		
8		
9		
10		

Draw a 'light and shade' map of the school grounds.

Can you suggest reasons for your findings?

Chapter 3 Plant Energy

Plants use energy from the sun to produce their own food and to grow. This process is called photosynthesis. This chapter will suggest activities to help pupils to look at how plants get their power and how we can make use of it.

Plants as solar collectors

Introduce children to the idea of plants as solar collectors. Plants collect energy from the sun and use it, with water, carbon dioxide and nutrients from the soil, to produce their own food. Look carefully at different kinds of plants. Compare the size and shapes of their leaves.

Take three plants, grown in pots from seed, such as tomatoes or chillies. Treat all three exactly the same, with the same sized pots, measured amounts of water, any plant food, equal temperatures. Put one in a dark cupboard, put one in a shady place, and the other on a sunny windowsill. Observe what happens over a week or two, recording observations on a daily basis. Ask the children to explain their results. They could then do similar experiments varying the other things plants need.

Map of solar collectors

Make a map of your school grounds to show the solar collectors - the different trees, bushes and other plants. How much of the surface of the grounds is covered in solar collectors? You could use squared paper or dimensions to work out the percentage of the area devoted to energy collection. Then ask difficult questions, such as whether some areas have more than one layer of solar collectors - for example trees with several layers of branches and grass growing underneath.

Plants store energy

If plants need the light, how do small seeds sown in the earth grow up above the soil? How do bulbs grow, even when you put them in a dark cupboard over winter? Explain that seeds and some plants which have bulbs or tubers (such as potatoes) store energy. They can begin to grow in the dark using their stored energy. Often the parts of plants we eat are the energy stores, such as carrots, potatoes, yams, wheat seeds.

Try growing new plants from old energy stores, such as a carrot top in a saucer, or a potato in a pot of soil.

Killing weeds

You can use the fact that plants need light to kill weeds. Cover the ground with something that excludes light, such as old sheets of cardboard, carpets or black plastic, to kill off weeds. Compare the effects of excluding light on perennial weeds, such as dandelion and couch grass, and annual weeds, such as chickweed. Why can perennial weeds live so much longer without light ? Compare the root systems of the different kinds of weeds. You could grow a dandelion in a jar with a collar over the top to observe the root system.

Beans in a jar

Children can grows beans in jam jars on a windowsill. They can take measurements of growth for the different parts of the plant and keep a diary of observations about the plant's development. Which part grows first and where does its energy come from? How soon do leaves develop? How fast do different parts grow?

Investigating trees' leaves

Use mirrors to look up at the canopies of different trees. Mirror tiles can be mounted onto plywood, or hand-held mirrors can be used. These give children a new way of seeing a tree as a series of layers around a central axis. This is a good way to begin thinking about the arrangement of leaves, their shapes and sizes and their orientation. Children can make drawings of what they see in the mirror. They can also think about how much of the area seen in the mirror is sky and how much is covered by leaves. Does this change as the children walk outwards from the trunk?

Other questions to ask about tree leaves are:

▶ Why are leaves so thin?

▶ Are some leaves better at collecting light than others because of their design? Look at different types and shapes of leaves, shiny and dull leaves, etc.

▶ Why do some leaves have holes?

Looking at one particular tree, ask:

▶ Are the leaves in one layer around the tree, or are they multi-layered?

▶ Do the leaves overlap?

▶ What angle are the leaves held at? (Twigs in shade usually hold their leaves horizontally to obtain the most light, but twigs in sun hold their leaves at many different angles.)

▶ What sizes of leaves are found where on the tree?

▶ Are outer leaves more indented so that inner leaves can receive more sunlight? (Oak is often a good example of this.)

Fig 15. Killing weeds

Black plastic sheeting pegged or weighted down over a weedy patch will kill all the weeds.

Fig 16. Beans in a jar

Runner beans grow very easily given moisture, warmth and light. A roll of newspaper pushed into a jar with a little water in it traps some bean seeds between the glass and the paper. These will germinate in a few days.

Plant fuels

There are two types of plant fuels: renewable and non-renewable. Non-renewable energy comes from the sun indirectly. It has been stored in dead plants which changed into fossil fuels millions of years ago and is now found in rocks in the ground. When these fossil fuels have been used up they cannot be replaced. Renewable energy from plants usually comes in the form of wood or charcoal, which can be replaced by planting trees, but also includes oils. (See page 25.)

Fig 17. Plants in energy chains

A number of everyday examples of energy transfer through food chains can be observed in the school grounds. Children can record their findings as pictograms (see below).

Answering these questions will help to build up the idea that trees use their leaves to produce food. If this is the case, what happens in the winter when some trees lose their leaves?

Lengths of growing seasons and day-length

Plants in Britain are affected by the length of the growing season and by day-length. Although the growing season is determined by temperature, this is indirectly related to the Earth's movements in relation to the sun. Day-length affects plant growth too. Ask the children if they can devise an experiment to measure the effects of day-length on plant growth. What other factors will they have to control? How long will the experiment have to run for? Could they artificially control a plant's day-length?

Plants move towards the sun

Try an experiment to show this. Take a teaspoon of alfalfa seeds and soak them overnight. Place them on a moist paper towel in a tray or clear jar on a sunny windowsill. After a few days observe and record which way the plants are facing. Move the container so that the plants' leaves are facing away from the sun. Keep watch every half hour. How long is it before the leaves are facing the sun again?

You can investigate this further using other fully grown plants such as house plants, or vegetables in pots.

sun → leaves → caterpillar → blackbird → cat

sun → flower pollen → bee → bird → honey → me

Plants as food

Energy chains

Investigate which plants in the school grounds are eaten by which animals. This can be done by a combination of observation and using reference books. Don't forget to include any plants which can be eaten by humans. This can be developed from or into work on food chains. Can you construct some food chains for the school grounds? Food chains are also energy chains. Begin each of these chains with the sun. Ask children how else plants are used for energy apart from as food? This can lead on to work on fuels, such as wood and fossil fuels. (See pages 22 to 24.)

Composting

Investigate how dead plant materials are broken down by small animals such as beetles and worms. The animals feed on the plants. The plants provide them with energy. Children can even see this process taking place when the animals are micro-organisms, too small to be seen, by making a 'hot' compost heap.

Take a large quantity of different materials suitable for composting, such as mown grass, vegetable kitchen waste, shredded newspaper, animal manure and bedding, mix it all together and put it into a compost bin (about 1m x 1m is ideal). The material should be moist and preferably should fill the bin. Put the lid on and leave it. Measure the temperature of the material every day, or perhaps even twice a day. Use a soil thermometer if possible. The temperature should increase rapidly over the first few days, stabilise for a few days and then begin to fall. It may reach as high as 65° to 70°C.

Once the temperature begins to fall you can mix up the material in the heap, turning that from the sides into the middle to increase the temperature again. The heat is energy given off by the micro-organisms feeding on the plant material. They are actively decomposing the material. Once the heap cools down larger animals such as worms begin their work in the decomposition process.

Once the heap is ready (it looks like pleasant, brown, friable soil), it can be spread on or dug into the ground to feed plants. The compost is a source of energy. Some of the energy in the original plants has been used up by the soil organisms. Some of it is left as soil nutrients to be taken up by plants through their roots.

Fossil fuel audit

Do a 'fossil fuel audit' at school or in pupils' homes. Ask children to brainstorm the different ways in which energy is used at school. Make sure the children know what fuels are and what fossil fuels are. Then ask children to formulate questions they will need to ask to find out about the use of fossil fuels at school: e.g. What fuel is used in the central heating? What fuels are used to make mains electricity? What about teacher's cars? Can the children find a way to estimate how much of each kind of fossil fuel is used in a year?

Lead children on to thinking about other ways in which the school consumes energy in the products it uses. Is there any consumption of fossil fuel when they use paper or pens, or plastic containers? Get them to think about the energy used to make things, in manufacture, packaging and transport, etc. They won't be able to quantify this, but it would make an interesting subject for a large wall display showing all the different ways in which their classroom or school uses fossil fuel. You could perhaps use a large photograph of the classroom or school

Fig 18. Building a charcoal clamp

First a central chimney is constructed to allow air in.

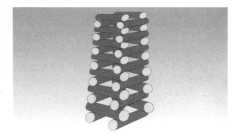

Then branches are laid against and around the chimney.

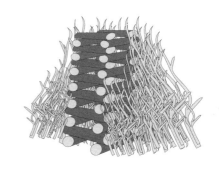

The wood clamp is made larger. More pieces of wood are laid on top.

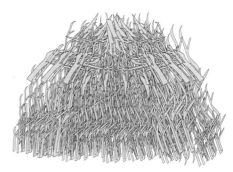

The finished clamp is covered with soil and grass.

as the centre, with lines coming out from the different fossil fuel consumers to explanations or diagrams.

Biofuels

These are living or recently living plant and animal products that provide energy. We will look at animal products in Chapter 4. Biofuels are renewable sources of energy as long as we replace them as fast as we use them. The main plant biofuels include wood, charcoal, oil crops such as rapeseed oil, or **Jatropha curcus**, other crops and waste materials such as sawdust, bark, etc. from sawmills. Burning of biofuels can be sustainable if more plants are grown, so soaking up the carbon dioxide produced when the fuel is burnt.

Bonfires

While bonfires, using wood, use renewable energy, they also give off carbon dioxide into the atmosphere and further increase the greenhouse effect. However, November is a good time to consider these issues. Children might like to visit a bonfire while it is being built to see what kinds of things are put on it. Could any of these things be recycled, or burnt in a home for heating to replace fossil fuel so saving energy ? After bonfire night you could discuss the heat given out by bonfires and how it might be be better used.

Charcoal burning clamp

Most children will have encountered charcoal being burnt at summer barbecues, but do they know how it is made? In some areas it is possible to visit charcoal burners to watch the process. Alternatively there is an excellent passage in **'Swallows and Amazons'** by Arthur Ransome. You could try to make your own charcoal in the school grounds, and it is possible to produce small amounts of drawing charcoal in a small clamp. Begin by building a small fire of dry twigs and once your bonfire is going well, cover it with turves of grass. Keep children well away at this stage as it will smoke. Make sure air can enter from the base. Then leave it to cool. When it has cooled there should be some charcoal at the bottom.

Locality studies

Compare the sources of energy used in your school or homes, with that in the contrasting locality you are studying in geography. If you are studying India or Nepal, or Kenya or most other parts of Africa, the problem of shortage of wood fuel is a major one for the people living there. The United Nations estimates that 3000 million people will be short of firewood by the year 2000. While wood may be a renewable energy source, population pressures coupled with inefficient wood use have caused considerable deforestation, and wood fires are polluting. In the past people used to collect dead wood for their fires, but increasingly that is not possible. Wood is only renewable if replacement trees are planted.

Children could find out about fuel-efficient stoves such as the jikos used in Kenya. Ask them to think about what makes a stove efficient. How could their electric or gas stove at home be used more efficiently? Is a barbecue an efficient way to cook food? They could do an experiment comparing the fuel efficiency of a microwave oven with a barbeque and a conventional oven. They could even compare with a solar oven (see page 14). Compare the cost of the fuel and length of cooking time. Then also discuss the advantages and disadvantages of the different methods for different situations - pollution, reliability of supplies, cost of oven itself and energy consumed in making it.

Safety warning: take care to keep children away from fire and smoke.

Fig 19. Jiko stove

Wood or charcoal is burnt in the bottom of the stove. A jiko uses 75% of the wood used by an open fire. Insulated jikos have now been developed to increase efficiency.

Cooking pot

Firebox

Plant oils

Plant oils such as groundnut (peanut) oil provide us with energy via our food. But plant oils can also provide energy in other ways. If you are doing Victorian Britain in history, talk about oil lamps. If possible, borrow a working oil lamp and demonstrate it for the children. If you are studying the Romans the children could construct small clay Roman oil lamps, and then some could be filled with olive oil and lit.

Investigate what kinds of fruits and seeds produce oil. Visit the supermarket and make a list of all the different oils. Try crushing sesame, sunflower or other seeds in a pestle and mortar. Find out the amount of oil in different types of seeds. Crush them on to paper and hold it up to the light to see the mark. Measure the mark. Devise a fair test for this.

Alternative plant fuels

Sugar cane and sugar beet both store energy in the form of sugar and can be made into fuel. In Brazil and Kenya sugar is converted into gasohol and used to run cars.

Some countries use by-products from other processes to generate electricity. For example Mauritius gets 10% of its electricity from burning the stems of sugar cane plants. In the Netherlands and Germany electricity is produced by burning household rubbish in large incinerators. In Sweden refuse is burnt to provide hot water and heating for houses. Electricity can also be produced from the methane gas given off from landfill sites. Methane adds to the greenhouse effect, and burning landfill gas both removes the harmful methane, and releases less carbon dioxide than burning fossil fuels would. Help the children to investigate whether their local authority has any plans to produce electricity in these ways. Are there any waste products available locally in large quantities? Could dairy farms or sewage works use the methane they produce to power their equipment?

Fig 20. Roman oil lamp

A simple oil lamp made from clay. Pour in some oil and check that the lamp does not leak. Soak the wick in oil and put that into the hole, with a little wick protruding. Light the wick. How long does it burn?

Safety warning: take care with burning oil lamps.

Seed power

In some parts of West Africa, Jatropha curcus, a euphorbiaceous shrub, is grown. Its seeds produce an oil which can be used instead of diesel. The seeds have 30% oil content and the oil can be extracted with a simple press. In Mali the oil is used to power food processing machines.

Chapter 4 Animal Energy

Animals get their energy or power indirectly from the sun by eating plants and/or other animals. In thinking about animal power it is useful to think about where it comes from - food chains, what we eat, which foods give us most energy, etc. and how we use or can measure it. Comparisons might be made with other sources of energy such as batteries, petrol or diesel, looking at cost and convenience and other factors such as use of fossil fuels and pollution. Human and animal energy is renewable energy.

In animals chemical energy is provided directly from food or from fat and glycogen (the glucose store) in the body. When the muscles contract and relax this changes chemical energy to mechanical energy. Part of the energy changed in this way is used by the muscles, the rest is released as heat.

Food chains for plants and animals

Paper chains

Make paper chains to show the food chains from plants to animals, but starting from the sun. This could be done by groups of children. Challenge the more able children to make chains which include as many different types of organisms as possible. You could hang all the chains beginning at the central light in your classroom (a symbolic sun) and radiating out.

Fig 21. Paper food chains

Each link in these Christmas-style paper chains represents a link in the food chain, and each starts with the sun.

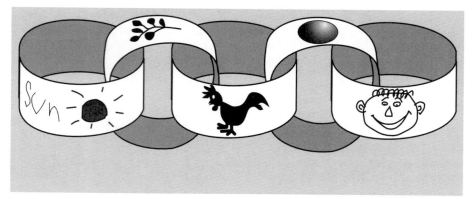

Energy chains in the school grounds

Investigate the energy flows and draw energy chains for animals in the school environment, for example, birds in the grounds. Where does their energy come from? How do they use it? Think about their activities, such as feeding, walking, flying, keeping warm. They could be shown at the end of the chain.

Animals' food

Growth monitoring of small animals

Growing animals use much of the food (chemical energy) they eat for growth. Watch caterpillars feeding on cabbage or nasturtium leaves. If possible bring some into the classroom and put one small caterpillar on one large leaf in order to be able to see the amount eaten. Measure the caterpillar at the beginning and then every day as it grows until it changes into a chrysalis. Ask the children to think about all the things it uses its energy for.

How much do animals eat?

Let children investigate how much animals eat: pets, farm animals or wild animals. What kinds of foods do different animals like? Visit a pet shop and find out about the food needs of different animals, or do a survey of class pets. Which foods are likely to provide most energy? Compare the labels of proprietory foods, for example for cats and dogs.

Go on from this to ask other questions, such as:

▶ How do animals store energy?

▶ How do animals hibernate? - How do their bodies manage without food for long periods?

▶ Do animals vary in how they use energy? For example compare a cheetah or other large cat, with something which moves slowly, but most of the time.

▶ How does the amount an animal eats in weight compare with its body weight?

Working animals

Remind children of horse and donkey rides on the beach or at fairs. A working animal such as a donkey or horse can be thought of as a 'machine' which converts food (chemical energy) into work (mechanical energy). The food is also used by the animal for growth, health and other things. When the animal moves some energy is used by the muscles and some is released as heat. Children could investigate the following:

▶ which animals are used to provide power in Britain and in their contrasting locality in geography;

▶ in which kinds of situations and environments animals are most useful for power;

▶ how animal power was used in Britain in the historical period they are studying.

Even in urban areas it is possible to find working animals, as heavy horses are often kept by breweries. Invite someone who uses working animals to visit the school with their animals, or go and visit them. Discuss, and then compile a table to show the advantages and disadvantages of horse-and-cart transport in comparison with motor vehicles.

Horse-power

We sometimes talk about the horse-power of an engine or car. This is a unit of power - 550 ft-pounds per second. It was invented by James Watt. He found a strong horse could raise a weight of 150 pounds 4 feet in one second. The Watt is a metric unit of power, named after him. Children could investigate the horse-power of different vehicles and other machines in work on the history of transport and Britain in the early twentieth century.

Calories and joules

A calorie is a unit of energy. It is the same as the amount of heat needed to raise one gram of water 1°C. A Kilocalorie (also called a Calorie, capital 'C', or Kcal) is 1000 calories. It is often used to express the energy value of foods. A calorie is 4.18688 joules. A Calorie or Kcal is 4186.8 joules. A joule is the international metric unit of work or energy. It is equal to the work done when the point of application of 1 newton (a unit of force) moves through a distance of 1 metre.

Human food and energy

Food kilometres

The teacher could bring a bag of shopping into the classroom. The children list the items and then look at the packets to see what country they come from. It may be possible to work out that some ingredients come from other, different places. For example, chocolate made in the UK will contain cocoa from elsewhere, perhaps West Africa. Children can look up these places in an atlas and make a large world map on the wall to show where our food comes from.

Use an atlas to work out the distances in kilometres which different foods have travelled. Give a short list of foods to each group or pair of children. Then come together at the end to compare the distances. Which food has travelled furthest? Ask the children to consider whether the energy consumed in the journey was greater than that in the food itself. Some of the distances may be considerable underestimates. For example, tell the story of the Greek yogurt, made in Greece from milk produced in Britain, and then returned here. How many miles has it travelled? How much energy has been used in transport? Ask children to think about how they can find out how many litres of diesel are needed to carry a typical truck one kilometre. Then there are also considerations such as pollution and traffic congestion.

Ask the children to think also about the energy used in making the food (including making chemical fertilisers and powering irrigation), packaging the food and making the packaging, and transporting the food to the supermarket. Which foods are 'energy heavy' in the sense that they have used up lots of energy? Rank the foods in order or put them into categories related to energy use.

Energy labels on food packets

Look closely at different food packets and compare the weight of food contained in them with the amount of energy they provide (Kcals). What kinds of foods provide most energy per gram? Contrast high energy foods, such as sugar, or fats, with lower energy foods such as lettuce. Remind children that we need lots of other things such as minerals, vitamins and fibre for our bodies to work at their best. Some foods release energy slowly and these are better for us than those, like sweets, which provide instant energy but little else.

High energy drinks

Look at the labels of canned and bottled drinks. Are so-called 'high-energy' drinks really higher in energy than others? Compare the energy in Kcals in the container with the quantity of drink to work out the energy per ml. Then draw up a table to show the differences. Look at cost and test taste too. Which drink has most calories per ml? Which drink has least? Which is the best value in terms of energy? Which is best in terms of taste?

Fig 22. Food labels

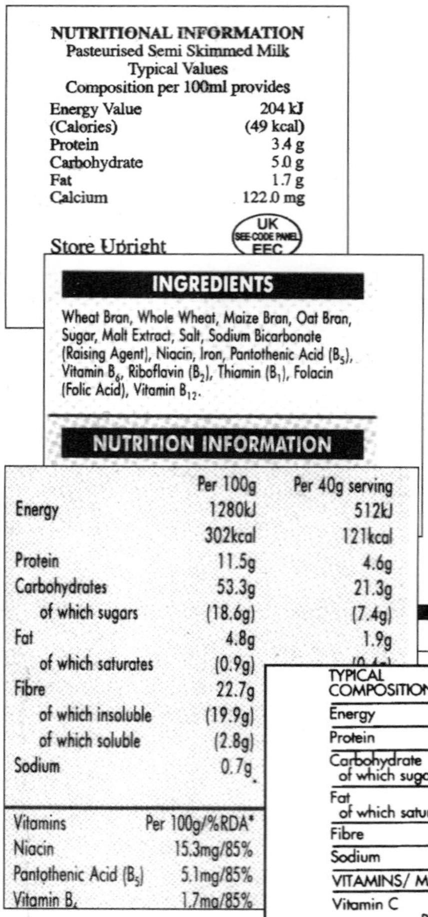

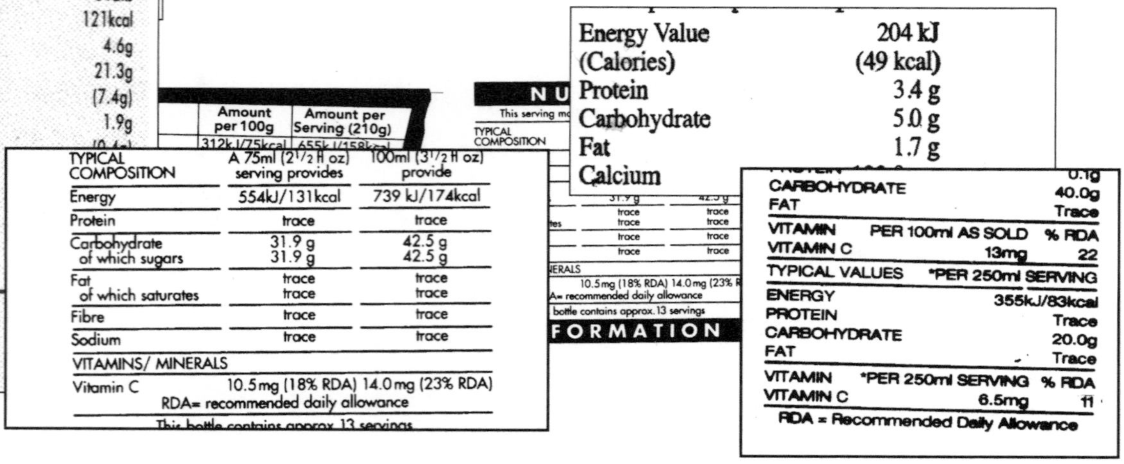

NUTRITIONAL INFORMATION
Pasteurised Semi Skimmed Milk
Typical Values
Composition per 100ml provides

Energy Value	204 kJ
(Calories)	(49 kcal)
Protein	3.4 g
Carbohydrate	5.0 g
Fat	1.7 g
Calcium	122.0 mg

Store Upright

INGREDIENTS

Wheat Bran, Whole Wheat, Maize Bran, Oat Bran, Sugar, Malt Extract, Salt, Sodium Bicarbonate (Raising Agent), Niacin, Iron, Pantothenic Acid (B₅), Vitamin B₆, Riboflavin (B₂), Thiamin (B₁), Folacin (Folic Acid), Vitamin B₁₂.

NUTRITION INFORMATION

	Per 100g	Per 40g serving
Energy	1280kJ	512kJ
	302kcal	121kcal
Protein	11.5g	4.6g
Carbohydrates	53.3g	21.3g
of which sugars	(18.6g)	(7.4g)
Fat	4.8g	1.9g
of which saturates	(0.9g)	
Fibre	22.7g	
of which insoluble	(19.9g)	
of which soluble	(2.8g)	
Sodium	0.7g	

Vitamins	Per 100g/%RDA*	
Niacin	15.3mg/85%	
Pantothenic Acid (B₅)	5.1mg/85%	
Vitamin B₆	1.7mg/85%	

TYPICAL COMPOSITION	A 75ml (2¹/₂ fl oz) serving provides	100ml (3¹/₂ fl oz) provide
Energy	554kJ/131kcal	739 kJ/174kcal
Protein	trace	trace
Carbohydrate	31.9 g	42.5 g
of which sugars	31.9 g	42.5 g
Fat	trace	trace
of which saturates	trace	trace
Fibre	trace	trace
Sodium	trace	trace
VITAMINS/ MINERALS		
Vitamin C	10.5mg (18% RDA)	14.0mg (23% RDA)

RDA= recommended daily allowance
This bottle contains approx. 13 servings

	Amount per 100g	Amount per Serving (210g)
	312k J/75kcal	655k J/158kcal

TYPICAL COMPOSITION		
Energy Value	204 kJ	
(Calories)	(49 kcal)	
Protein	3.4 g	
Carbohydrate	5.0 g	
Fat	1.7 g	
Calcium		

CARBOHYDRATE	40.0g	
FAT	Trace	
VITAMIN	PER 100ml AS SOLD	% RDA
VITAMIN C	13mg	22
TYPICAL VALUES	*PER 250ml SERVING	
ENERGY	355kJ/83kcal	
PROTEIN	Trace	
CARBOHYDRATE	20.0g	
FAT	Trace	
VITAMIN	*PER 250ml SERVING	% RDA
VITAMIN C	6.5mg	11
RDA = Recommended Daily Allowance		

Energy for a school meal

Find out about the energy used to produce a typical school meal. Draw a flow chart, like Fig 23 on page 30, to show all the ways in which energy has been used to produce the meal. Children will need to consider a number of points:

▶ the energy in the food itself and how it got there - animal and plant;

▶ the energy used in farming and harvesting the food;

▶ the energy used to change the plant or animal material into the food ingredients, before it got to the school, e.g. wheat to flour at a mill;

▶ the energy used in cooking;

▶ the energy used in transport, storing and freezing;

▶ the energy used by the school cooks.

Then ask children to think about or find out about the energy sources of the different foods and stages/processes. It would be useful to compare raw fresh foods with highly processed ones, perhaps from abroad. Which foods are likely to have used up least fossil fuels on their way to the pupils' stomachs?

At home children can draw a similar energy flow diagram for a meal at the weekend or evening.

Our own energy

Ask the children how they can find out what method of movement over a given distance, say 50 or 100 metres, takes the most energy. They could select movements such as hopping, skipping, running, jumping with feet together. Get them to think about the problems and variables involved. Does the speed matter? Can they use one person to test the different methods in succession? What are the problems of using several different people? Are there any ways they can think of to reduce these problems, for example by testing many times and averaging the results?

This is a complex problem, but might be helped by thinking about whether the same weight is being transported the same distance and asking the children to draw the path of movement.

Human energy audit

Ask children to shadow an adult for a day noting the different kinds of activity they engage in. It is best to record the activities in set categories. They must be careful to record the length of time the person does each activity for. See the photocopiable sheet, page 32.

	Women	Men
Cycling	192	256
Eating	84	112
Sitting in office	120	160
Sitting resting (watching TV)	84	112
Swimming	230	300
Walking	168	224

The hourly Calories (Kcal) required by different activities. Note these are for adult men and women.

Fig 23. Energy chart for a meal

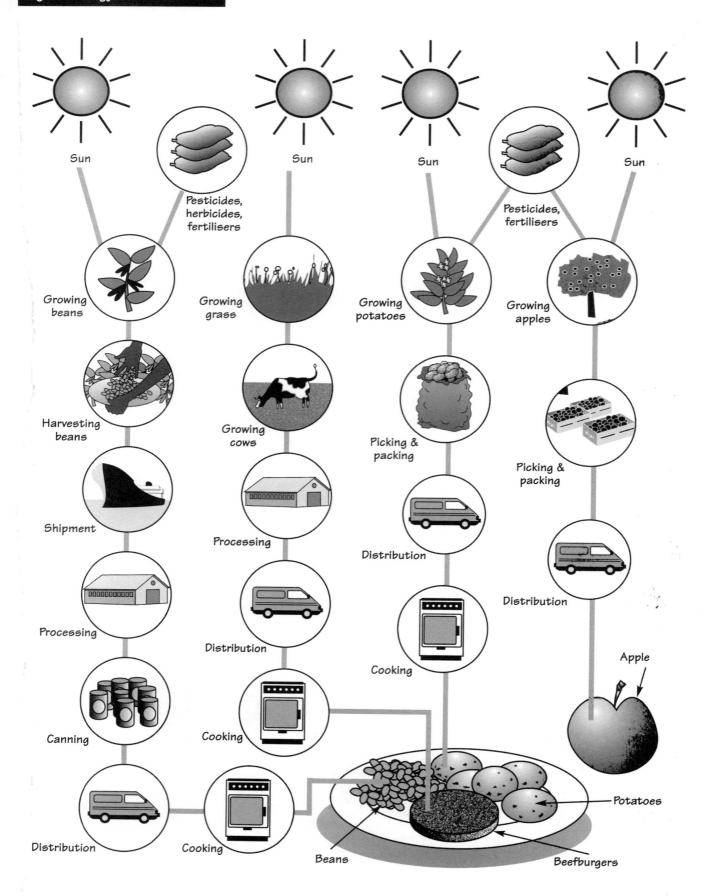

Human power

An easy experiment to determine the power output required for a particular exercise might be tackled as follows. The equipment required is a box suitable for 'step aerobics' type exercise, a ruler, a set of weighing scales and a watch with a second hand. Each child can do step aerobic exercises for a timed minute using the box. With W = weight of the child(Kg), U = number of upsteps onto the box and H = height of the box(m), the rate of work in Watts is determined by: W x U x H x 1/6. Each child might like to do the best of three attempts. A class average could be established. To convert the results to horse-power, divide Watts by 746.

Investigate the most energy efficient way of moving something large, such as a plastic box of books, from one end of the school grounds to the other. Can the children devise an experiment?

Clockwork and elastic band power

Look carefully at some clockwork and elastic-band powered toys or other things, for example a clockwork clock or one of the new clockwork radios with a transparent case.

▶ How long do they run for?

▶ Where does the power come from?

▶ How is the energy stored?

▶ Why is the clockwork radio such an important invention to people in Africa?

▶ Why do we now use battery powered watches and clocks rather than clockwork ones? What are the advantages and disadvantages?

Challenge the children to make a small elastic band powered toy which moves along a surface.

Bicycles and gears

Investigate why it takes less energy to cycle the same distance as to walk it. How do gears work? Why is it useful to have different gears on a bicycle? Could we use 'pedal power' for things other than moving from A to B? Children could use their imaginations to invent or design their own 'pedal power' machines to do other things. This could either be done on paper, or by making junk models, or even trying some ideas out using an old bicycle in the classroom.

Make sure that the children lift things safely, and that asthmatic children are taken into account during these experiments.

Fig 24. Elastic band powered vehicle

Cut a 12mm (approx) length of white wax candle with a sharp knife, and bore a hole through the middle with a hot skewer. While the skewer is still hot melt a furrow across the diameter on one end of the candle piece. Push a suitable elastic band through the cotton reel, (which must have flat ends), slide half a matchstick through the loop at one end and anchor this to the cotton reel using a thumbtack or glue. Thread the other end of the band through the piece of candle with the furrowed face outermost, and slide a matchstick through the loop. Bed the match into the furrow and turn the match and candle drive mechanism to twist the band and store the driving energy. Place on a flat surface.

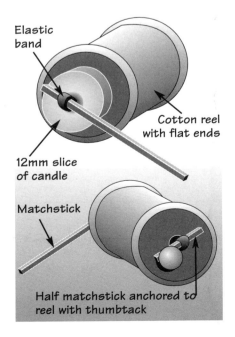

Elastic band

Cotton reel with flat ends

12mm slice of candle

Matchstick

Half matchstick anchored to reel with thumbtack

Energy used in 24 hours

Date

Activity	Time spent (hours)	Calories used
sleep		
rest		
watching TV		
reading/paper work		
other		
gentle exercise		
slow walking		
shopping		
cooking		
other		
vigorous exercise		
running		
playing sport		
riding a bicycle		
other		

Make sure the time adds up to 24 hours. Then add up the approximate number of calories used.

Chapter 5 Water Energy

When water is moving it has kinetic energy. This means that the water has energy because it is moving. Water power comes indirectly from the sun. The movement in rivers is caused by the sun acting on the atmosphere around the Earth. The sun causes water in the seas to evaporate and move upwards, and then to fall again as rain. The movement of the waves is caused by the winds, which are in turn caused by the sun. So the movements of the waves are indirectly caused by the sun. Tidal power is a little different in that it is caused mostly by the moon's movements.

A model of the water cycle

Make a model of the water cycle using a large baking pan or bowl, a piece of clear plastic film, a jam jar and weights. Half fill the bowl or pan with salt water. Stand the jam jar in the middle of the pan, empty, weighted down with a stone. Put the clear plastic across the top and weight the middle down. Stand the model in the sun. The sun's heat will cause water to evaporate from the 'sea'. As the air in the room is cooler than the air inside the solar collector, water will condense on the underside of the plastic sheet. It should then run down the underside of the sheet and drip into the jam jar. Ask the children to test whether the water in the jam jar is salty. Can they explain why not? Relate this to the difference between sea water and rain, and to the way the water cycle works.

Experimenting with water pressure

Water pressure is the force used to turn turbines and produce hydro-electric power. The amount of water pressure depends on the 'head'. This is the height through which the water falls. The greater the 'head', the greater the water pressure and the more power produced.

Children can investigate the effect of the 'head' on the water pressure using two buckets and a length of plastic tube (such as that used for wine-making). Fill a bucket full of water and mark the level carefully. Put the bucket high up on a shelf, or outside, high on a wall. Put one end of the tube into the bottom of the bucket. Fill the tube completely with water and use your thumb on the end to form a siphon. Let the water flow through the tube into the other bucket. Use a stop watch or watch to time how long this takes. Try putting the full bucket at different heights above the empty one. Measure the heights. What variables affect the amount of time it takes for the same amount of water to flow down the tube? Ask the children to show their results in a table.

Fig 25. The water cycle

A baking pan, some cling film and a jam jar can be set up to model the Earth's weather system. The sun's energy vapourises the water in the pan which condenses on the plastic film and drops into the jam jar.

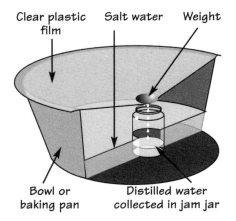

Clear plastic film   Salt water   Weight

Bowl or baking pan   Distilled water collected in jam jar

Turbines and water wheels

A model water-powered turbine

Turbines are used for generating electricity from water power. They need to rotate fast and usually need a high head of water. Make a model water turbine and try it out with a tube or hose connected to a tap.

Fig 26. Model turbine

A small turbine made with stiff card or plastic vanes set into a cork.

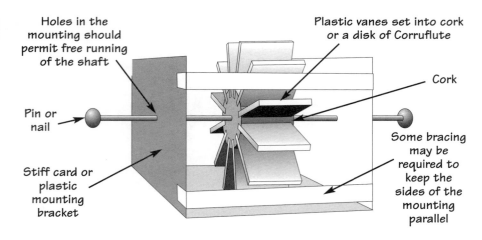

Holes in the mounting should permit free running of the shaft

Plastic vanes set into cork or a disk of Corruflute

Cork

Pin or nail

Some bracing may be required to keep the sides of the mounting parallel

Stiff card or plastic mounting bracket

The bucket and tube used above will not give enough power to make this work well, but it would be a good idea to try it for comparison. The bucket and tube will allow the children to measure the head as well as the flow rate.(Remind children that the water from the tap is being pumped along the pipes.) Compare the flow rates from tap and bucket. To measure the flow rate direct all the water into a container and time how long it takes to fill. Then divide the volume of water collected, by the time it took to fill. This is the flow rate, usually expressed in litres per second.

Use a short fat cork or a disk of Corruflute for the turbine and strong plastic for the holder and the fins. Fit the cork turbine to the holder using pins for axles. The faster the stream of water the faster the turbine will turn. Can the children think of a way of measuring how fast the turbine is turning?

A simple turbine

Make a simple water-powered turbine using a plastic bottle. Cut the top off the bottle and make holes around the sides, near the base. Angle the holes by placing a pencil in the hole and and pushing it against the side of the bottle. Then hang the bottle by a string and hold it under a running tap.This is best done outside if possible.

Fig 27. A simple turbine

The movement of a turbine comes from the transfer of kinetic energy from the water to the turbine. It is important that the holes are angled round, as described in the text, to make sure that the water jets exert a rotary force on the water container.

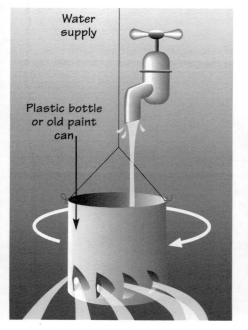

Water supply

Plastic bottle or old paint can

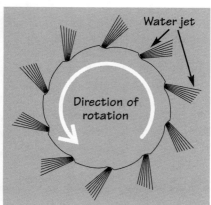

Water jet

Direction of rotation

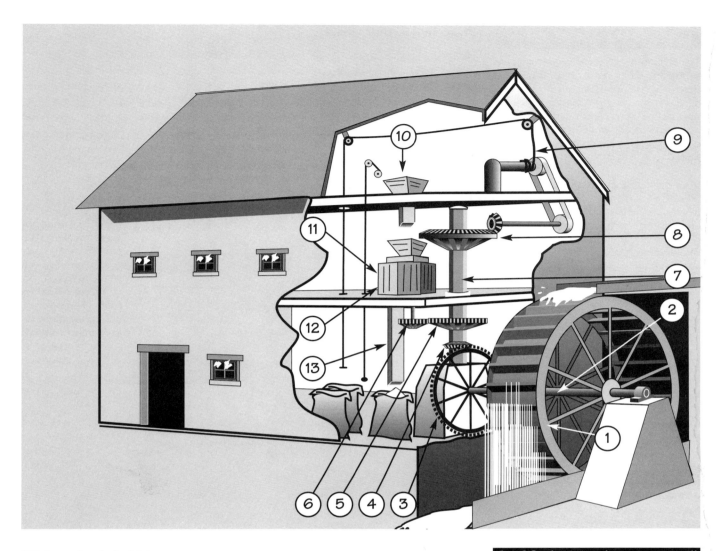

Water wheels in history

Investigate the history of water power in your area as part of a local history study, or related to whichever HSU is appropriate. In the past water wheels were very common and were used for grinding or milling flour, working bellows in forges, and running machinery in workshops. In 1086, the Domesday Book recorded 5600 water wheels in England. By the 19th century there were over 30,000 water mills in Britain. They were replaced by fossil fuelled engines of various kinds. In some areas there are working water mills which can be visited.

Water wheels are used for mechanical work, not usually for generating electricity. They turn fairly slowly but with a lot of force. Let children find out about different kinds of water wheels: undershot, overshot and Ghatta. Ask them to compare the advantages and disadvantages of using water wheels, compared with petrol or diesel engines to do the same job.

Fig 28. An overshot water mill

The main components of a water mill are shown above:

KEY:
1. Waterwheel
2. Horizontal shaft
3. Pitwheel
4. Wallower
5. Great spur wheel
6. Stone nut
7. Vertical shaft
8. Crown wheel
9. Chain hoist
10. Hopper
11. Runner stone (top)
12. Bed stone (bottom)
13. Flour chute

Fig 29. An overshot water wheel

The left hand diagram shows the water buckets (egg cups or cut-down plastic cups) stapled to the card discs. The right hand diagram shows how to measure the work potential of the wheel by attaching a load for it to wind upwards on the shaft.

Draw four diameters at 45° on one of the card discs to locate the eight egg cups (or cut down plastic cups) for stapling. The axle shaft can be a knitting needle (with the point filed off) or small diameter dowelling. The whole apparatus can be mounted on a stiff card or plastic frame similar to that shown in Fig 26 on page 34.

Make an overshot wheel

Overshot wheels need a small head of water, just a little higher than the height of the wheel. They can be used with a small volume of water. The weight of water in the buckets turns the wheel. The wheel turns slowly, but with great power. They were often used for grinding grain as considerable power was needed to turn the heavy grinding stones, and the speed had to be steady. The Persians used a wheel similar to the model shown below, using terracotta pots, for irrigation.

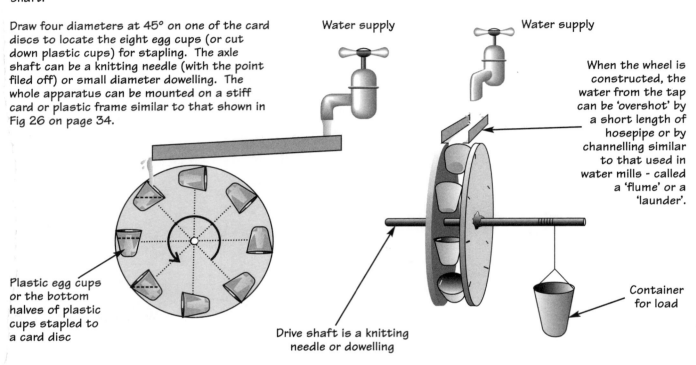

Water supply

Water supply

When the wheel is constructed, the water from the tap can be 'overshot' by a short length of hosepipe or by channelling similar to that used in water mills - called a 'flume' or a 'launder'.

Plastic egg cups or the bottom halves of plastic cups stapled to a card disc

Drive shaft is a knitting needle or dowelling

Container for load

Fig 30. An undershot water wheel

In an undershot wheel the movement of the water in a channel propels the blades of the wheel around. Use the same basic design as shown on previous pages but make up a channel from two blocks of wood glued and pinned to a piece of plywood.

Make an undershot wheel

Undershot or paddle wheels have been used for over 2000 years. The paddles dip down into a natural stream or man made channel. A simple paddle wheel design can be tried in a channel such as a piece of plastic drain pipe, using a hose to supply the water. Make the wheel using a cork or cotton reel and fins of plastic.

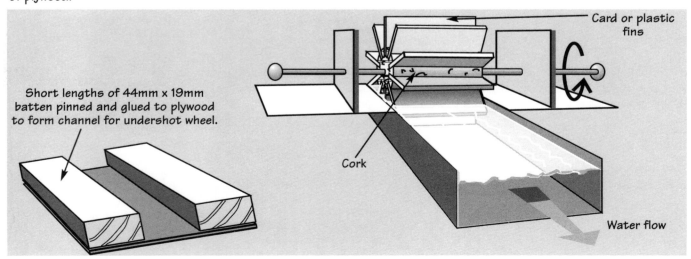

Card or plastic fins

Short lengths of 44mm x 19mm batten pinned and glued to plywood to form channel for undershot wheel.

Cork

Water flow

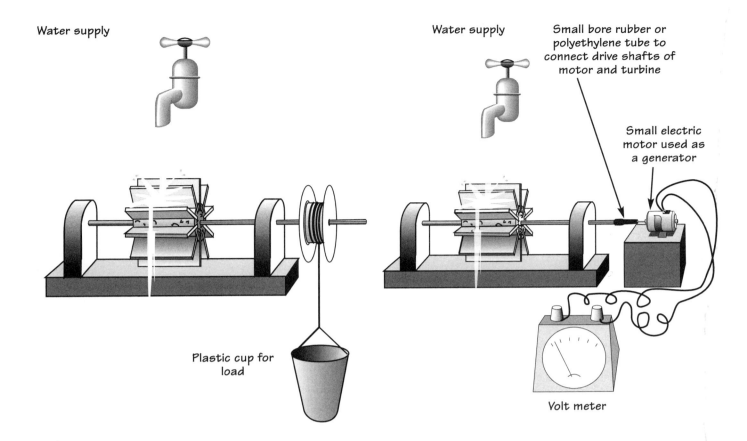

Water supply

Plastic cup for load

Water supply

Small bore rubber or polyethylene tube to connect drive shafts of motor and turbine

Small electric motor used as a generator

Volt meter

Investigate water power designs

Make a test rig to try out pupils' designs of water wheels and turbines. This might be placed in a large sink under a tap, or outside in a tank under an outside tap or hose. Use plastic for the main structure and arrange it so that different kinds of wheels and turbines can be used in it. To test water wheels, make them do mechanical work, such as lifting a weight or weights on a string. To test turbines you could produce electricity using a small electric motor. Most of the motors used in battery powered toys, and those for use in schools will work. You may be able to generate enough electricity to light a small bulb, but that is unlikely so you can test the output with a meter.

Let children try out different designs of wheels and turbines. Wheel bodies or hubs can be made from cork, cotton reels, plywood or plastic jar lids. Different kinds of fins can be made using flat pieces of plastic and curved pieces from old plastic bottles, also plastic spoons, bottle tops and tin foil food cartons. Shafts can be made from wooden dowel, plastic rod, old plastic knitting needles, or metal rods.

Fig 31. Test rig for power generation

These rigs can be used to compare the output for a number of different types and sizes or turbine or water wheel. It is important to remember to control the input factors (water flow for example) if comparisons are to be made of output levels.

Some typical designs of water wheels are also illustrated.

Fig 32. Different types of wheels and blades

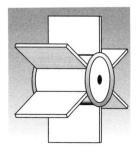

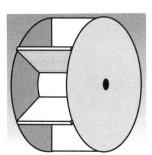

Water supply

Plastic container

Fig 33. Turbine in a bottle

A plastic milk or oil container with the base and one side cut out as shown provides an ideal mounting for a turbine as well as reducing splashing.

Fig 34. Measuring the head

The potential head of water for use in a water power system can be calculated using the simple apparatus shown here. Accuracy is not important unless the head is likely to be small, in which case more sophisticated surveying techniques would be required. The head = A + B

To avoid splashing and enable each group of children to build their own portable turbine, the turbines could be mounted in large plastic bottles. Large rectangular bottles are best, especially those used for mineral water, which are transparent. If you only have opaque ones available you could cut a hole in the side so that you can see what is happening.

Water power in your environment

Look at the area around the school to see whether any sites might be suitable for using water power, either today or in the past. Discuss with the pupils those things needed for water power production of different kinds and list them. Then look at local maps, as part of your geography study of the school locality. Are there any rivers or streams? Are there any slopes which would provide 'head' for generating electricity using turbines? Are there any sites marked as mills, or place names, such as Mill Lane? Are there any narrow valleys suitable for damming? Take a walk around the neighbourhood and look for evidence of water power and possibilities for new sites.

Set the challenge for pupils to decide on the best site for either a small scale hydro-electric scheme or a water wheel.

Measuring stream flow

As part of a study of a local stream, or work on possible water power sites, investigate the power of a local stream. For safety and practicality this needs to be a small, shallow stream. You could even construct a model stream in the school grounds, using guttering and a hose pipe, either as a test before tackling the real thing, or to measure flow on controlled slopes. There are several methods for measuring flow: for a very small stream, channel or hose, use the method described on page 34.

Measuring the head

When you are using a tap as a source of water there is no head because the water has been pumped and that is what gives it its force, rather than falling from a height. However, if you have a small stream nearby you could try to measure the head of that. Ask the children to think about what they need to measure and how they might do this. You will need to measure the height difference between the water surfaces at the inlet and outlet points. You can do this using a long spirit level and a long straight pole.

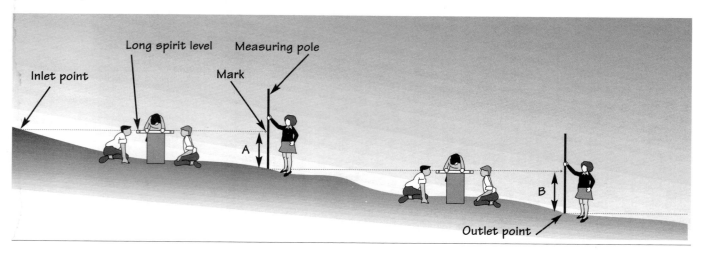

Inlet point

Long spirit level Measuring pole

Mark

A

B

Outlet point

Chapter 6 Wind Energy

Wind is moving air. The sun makes the air move and windmills take the energy from moving air, so indirectly wind power is solar power. Wind power activities might begin by looking at weather and climate, at how the sun causes winds, or perhaps as technology challenges.

Measuring the wind

Using the senses

Begin by getting children to use all their senses to experience the wind. Go outside and ask them to close their eyes and feel, perhaps even to smell the wind (are smells are coming from a particular direction, e.g. a factory?) Even on a day with a very light breeze they can feel the wind on their faces and hands, and in their hair. Ask them to listen to any sounds made by the wind. Finally, they can open their eyes and look for signs of the wind. Collect a list of everything everyone has noticed. This could be the basis for poems or stories about the wind.

Weather watch

Children can observe the wind for themselves and collect information using some of the instruments shown here. Don't forget to include observations such as watching washing on lines across a city from a tower block, or the direction of tree growth in seaside or mountainous areas. Discuss with children which way the prevailing winds blow. The children's own information or measurements can be compared with official statistics from the Met Office.

The wet finger test

Perhaps the simplest way of telling the wind direction, used by sailors, is to wet your finger and hold it up in the air. The side that is instantly coldest indicates the direction the wind is blowing from.

Wind socks

Children can make a simple wind sock by making a tunnel of thin, lightweight fabric and attaching it to a circle of wire and a stick. Children can experiment with different weights of fabric and other materials. How can they place the sock and mark the ground or surface to show the compass direction? Which places in the school grounds are windiest?

Experimenting with wind gauges and windmills can be dangerous. It is very important that blades are securely fixed before models are tested as even a small piece of card or plastic can do a lot of harm, flying through the air and hitting someone.

Fig 35. Wind sock

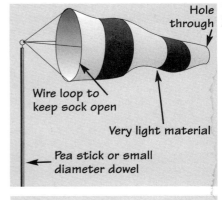

Hole through

Wire loop to keep sock open

Very light material

Pea stick or small diameter dowel

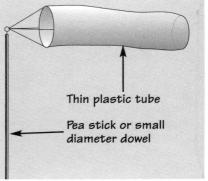

Thin plastic tube

Pea stick or small diameter dowel

Fig 36. Weather vanes

Observations of the direction and speed of the wind at particular locations lead to discussions on the best places for setting up wind power experiments.

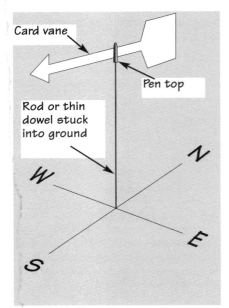

Card vane

Pen top

Rod or thin dowel stuck into ground

N

W

E

S

Make a simple arrow weather vane, as shown below, to show wind direction, or a weather vane which also indicates wind speed.

▶ 1. Use cardboard or plastic from large margarine or ice cream containers. Cut a circle about 15cm diameter to form the wheel.

▶ 2. Make cuts from the outside edge to about 3cm from the centre.

▶ 3. Bend the blades of the wheel to an angle of 45 degrees.

▶ 4. Make the tail vane from a piece of card folded in two for strength.

▶ 5. Attach the tail vane to the stick with a vertical pin in front of the broad part of the tail. (The vane needs to balance.)

▶ 6. Attach the wheel to the front of the tail vane with a pin or 'popped' rivet. You may need a bush to separate the wheel from the tail. Make sure the vane can rotate freely on the stick and that the wheel can rotate freely.

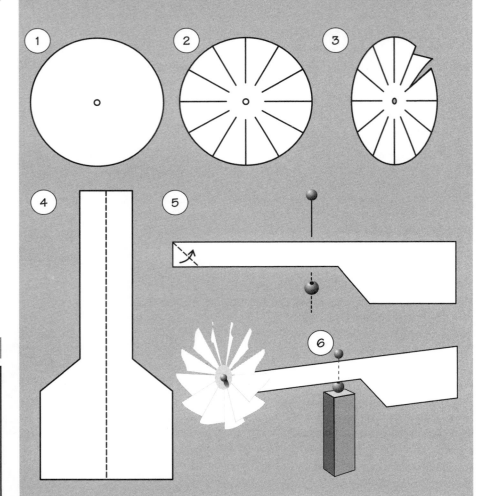

Making wind indoors

You may not want children to take all models and measuring instruments outdoors, especially at the design stage. Instead you could use an office fan to test designs, but adult supervision is essential. This works better than a hairdryer or a vacuum cleaner with an air blower.

Wind roses

Children can measure the wind direction every day for a month or more. This should give an idea of the prevailing wind. They can record their findings on a wind rose by shading, perhaps using different colours for different wind speeds, or by putting the date into the appropriate bar.

Wind speed

The strength or speed of the wind can be described simply as follows:

Wind Strength	Observed Effects
calm	smoke rises vertically
light breeze	wind felt on face, leaves rustle
moderate breeze	dust and loose paper rise, small branches move
strong breeze	large branches move
gale	twigs break off trees

Children could make their own wind scale chart with pictures showing the observed effects in their own environment.

Direction and speed indicators can be made in a variety of ways. The two examples consist of crepe paper streamers with knotted ends shown in Fig 38. The second version has different weight knots which acts as a primitive wind speed indicator.

Fig 37. A wind rose

Colour in one bar daily to record the direction of the wind over a given period.

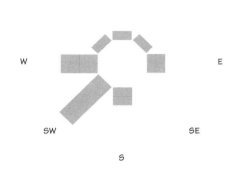

Fig 38. Wind speed and direction indicators

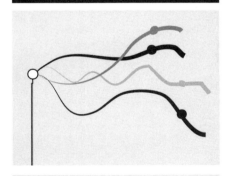

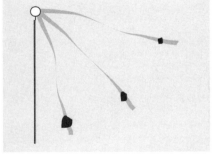

Beaufort scale

The Beaufort scale was invented by Sir Francis Beaufort in the early 19th century from observations of the effects of wind levels on fully rigged sailing ships. There are 13 levels to the scale from dead calm to hurricane:

Beaufort number (metres/second)	Description	Wind speed
0	calm	0.0 - 0.2
1	light air	0.3 - 1.5
2	light breeze	1.6 - 3.3
3	gentle breeze	3.4 - 5.4
4	moderate breeze	5.5 - 7.9
5	fresh breeze	8.0 - 10.7
6	strong breeze	10.8 - 13.8
7	near gale	13.9 - 17.1
8	gale	17.2 - 20.7
9	strong gale	20.8 - 24.4
10	storm	24.5 - 28.4
11	violent storm	28.5 - 32.6
12	hurricane	more than 32.7

Pinwheels

These are good simple instruments to show relative wind speeds. Ask children to experiment with different materials, sizes and types of pinwheels. Which works best? Challenge the children to find a way of counting the number of times the pinwheel turns in a given period of time. You could try a pinwheel with a shaft winding up a thread from a cotton reel as it rotates.

Fig 39. How to make pinwheels

These are easy to make and work well. The secret is to make sure the paper wheel does not foul on the stick or the pin. In general, it is best to use plastic or wooden beads (or a slice of drinking straw as shown here) as spacers to give adequate clearance for the wheel. 'A' (right) shows a pinwheel made from plastic or card vanes set into a cork hub. 'B' shows a simpler version which uses a square of light card or plastic cut and folded as shown.

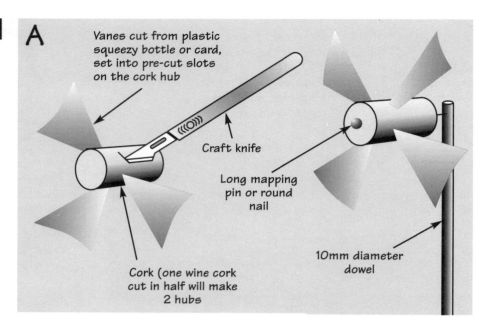

A

Vanes cut from plastic squeezy bottle or card, set into pre-cut slots on the cork hub

Craft knife

Long mapping pin or round nail

10mm diameter dowel

Cork (one wine cork cut in half will make 2 hubs

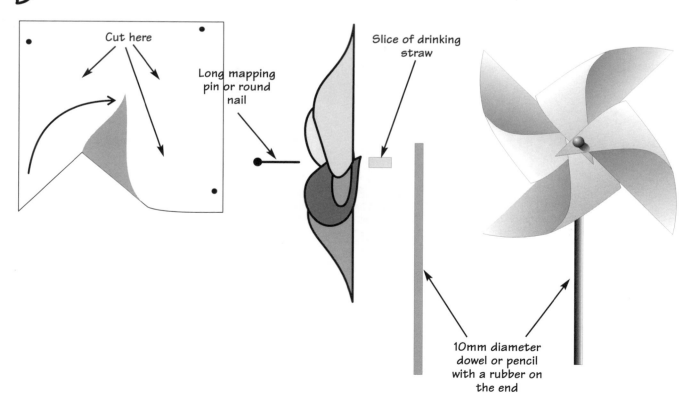

B

Cut here

Long mapping pin or round nail

Slice of drinking straw

10mm diameter dowel or pencil with a rubber on the end

Cup spinners

These spin round fast in the horizontal plane. The cups can be made from egg boxes, yogurt pots or paper cones. These are attached to dowelling arms and a pole. Compare cup spinners powered from an artificial source of wind, and outside in a natural wind.

Cloth strips

Cloth strips (without a selvage edge) will fray fastest where the wind is generally strongest so they are good for comparing the windiness at different sites, for example in the school grounds. Suspend each cloth strip from a pole set into the ground. Use the same type of material, suspended at the same height above the ground, to make a fair comparison between sites. It may also be possible to tell which sites are turbulent and at which the wind blows steadily, by observation.

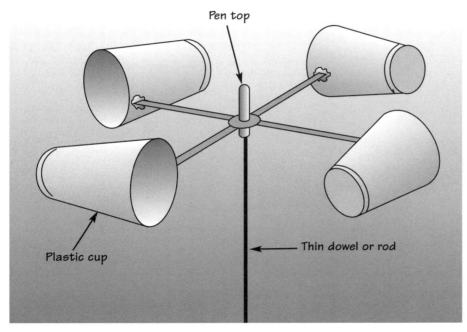

Pen top

Plastic cup

Thin dowel or rod

Fig 40. Cup spinners

These can be made from paper cones, plastic cups or egg box cups cut and stuck to wooden spills or thin dowel with tape or plastic glue gun. The pivot assembly is made from a suitable pen top resting over a straightened out wire coat hanger or rod. The balance of the spinner can be adjusted with blobs of glue or Plasticine to ensure free running.

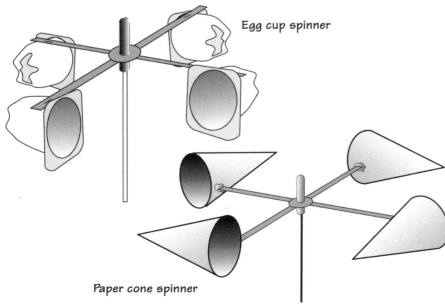

Egg cup spinner

Paper cone spinner

Wind gauges or anemometers

These measure wind speed. There are two fairly simple kinds of hand-held wind gauge which children can make themselves. One uses a piece of card suspended on a piece of dowel. The other uses a cardboard gauge with string or thread. Why not make both and compare their effectiveness? Can children design the best wind gauge for different types of wind conditions?

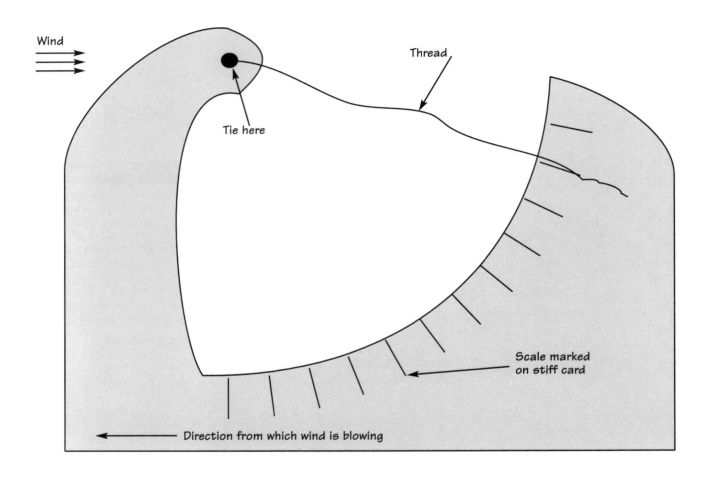

Wind

Thread

Tie here

Scale marked on stiff card

Direction from which wind is blowing

Fig 41. String and card wind gauges

1. Use this template (above) to cut a piece of cardboard.

2. Tie thread or string in a hole made near to the edge of the cardboard. Thread will move in a light breeze. String is better for a stronger breeze.

3. Move gauge until thread is blowing parallel to bottom of gauge. This shows wind direction.

4. Where the thread points along the arc shows relative speed.

Another design is shown on the facing page, using a protractor, stick, pin and piece of paper or cloth.

Relate the movement shown by the scale of your wind gauge to actual wind speeds by comparing your readings with that of a commercial anenometer. (These are available for as little as £10 from suppliers - see Resources.)

Wind map of school grounds

Use some of the instruments above, along with careful observation, to create a map of the school grounds showing windy and less windy areas. Readings will need to be taken on different days and at different times and then averaged. This map could then be the basis on which to decide where to site different objects or activities, such as wind power experiments, kite flying, badminton, rubbish bins, a vegetable bed, quiet corners, or where to build shelter belts.

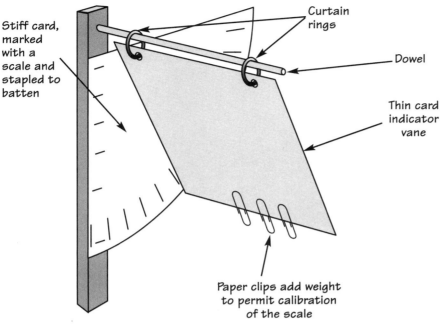

Stiff card, marked with a scale and stapled to batten

Curtain rings

Dowel

Thin card indicator vane

Paper clips add weight to permit calibration of the scale

Fig 42. Wind gauges

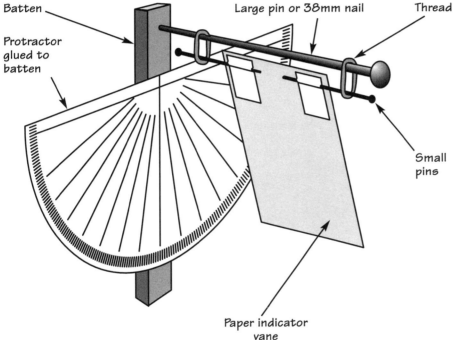

Batten

Protractor glued to batten

Large pin or 38mm nail

Thread

Small pins

Paper indicator vane

Litter and leaves

Ask children to note the places in the school grounds where litter and/or leaves collect. Compare these with places which are free of litter or leaves. Do these places change depending on the wind direction? Do they tell you anything about the prevailing winds, wind turbulence or sheltered areas?

Kites

Flying kites in the school grounds can help children find out about the winds. They also show the power of the wind at higher levels than we can feel. There are many different designs for kites. The one shown on page 46 is fairly easy for children to make and will fly well.

Experimenting with kites must always be supervised. Never fly a kite near telephone or power lines or in crowded places. Always wear gloves to prevent the kite line burning or cutting the children's hands.

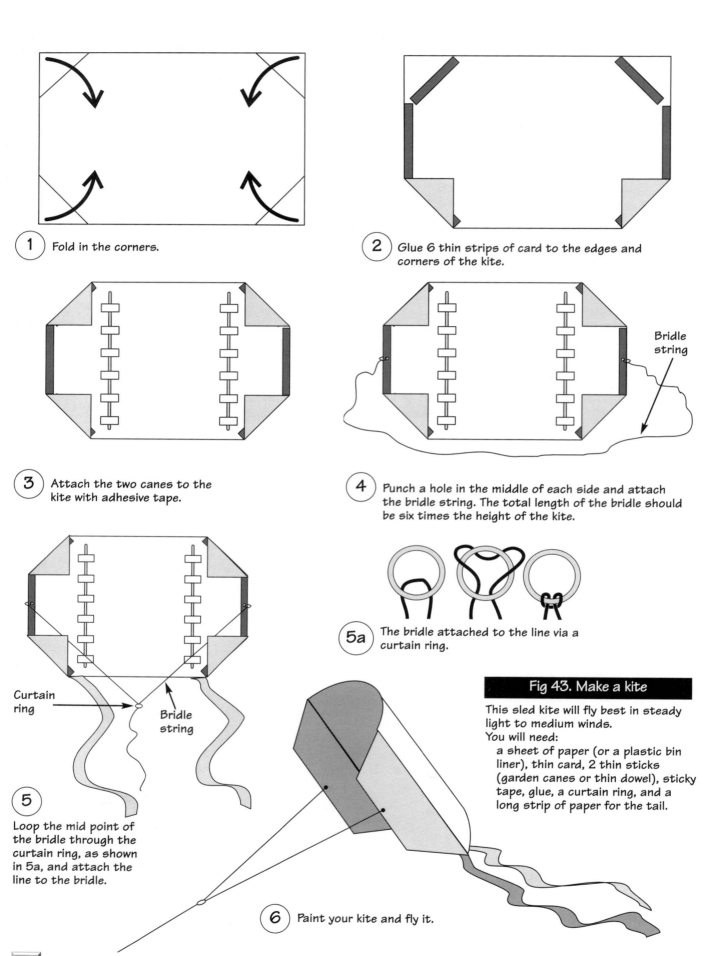

① Fold in the corners.

② Glue 6 thin strips of card to the edges and corners of the kite.

③ Attach the two canes to the kite with adhesive tape.

④ Punch a hole in the middle of each side and attach the bridle string. The total length of the bridle should be six times the height of the kite.

Bridle string

5a The bridle attached to the line via a curtain ring.

Curtain ring

Bridle string

⑤ Loop the mid point of the bridle through the curtain ring, as shown in 5a, and attach the line to the bridle.

⑥ Paint your kite and fly it.

Fig 43. Make a kite

This sled kite will fly best in steady light to medium winds.
You will need:
  a sheet of paper (or a plastic bin liner), thin card, 2 thin sticks (garden canes or thin dowel), sticky tape, glue, a curtain ring, and a long strip of paper for the tail.

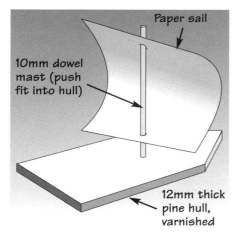

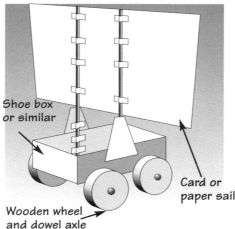

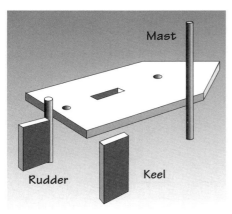

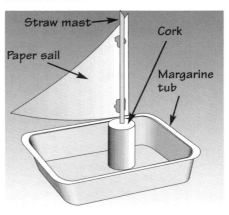

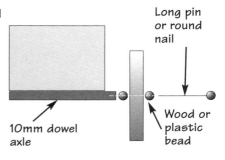

Fig 44. Model land yacht and sailing boats

Care should be taken in the construction of the running gear to avoid undue friction between the wheels and axle (see diagram below). For a boat the mast and sail should be as light as possible to prevent capsizing.

Challenge children to design different types of kites, using different shapes and materials. Which fly best? Which materials work best in different wind conditions? Hold a kite flying competition in the school grounds, with different categories - longest in the air, highest/longest string paid out, most interesting design, most aerobatic. It could even become an annual event and parents may like to be involved.

Yachts

Make model land yachts and investigate the best shapes of sails to power them. If you have a suitable pond or large sink or bath children might make simple sailing boats and investigate the best kinds of sails.

History of sailing ships

Investigate the history of sail power from early times through to the modern day as part of a historical study of transport through time. Visit a local sailing club or boat show, or use model boats on a pond or large tank. Help children to find out how sails worked to enable the ship to sail in different directions.

Moving scarecrows

An interesting technology challenge might be to use the power of the wind to protect crops from birds. Children will need to examine existing scarecrows. How can they make theirs more effective, perhaps by including moving parts, such as arms which spin in the wind, or a spinning hat? Different scarecrow designs can be tried out in the school grounds and used to protect the school garden. Which works best against the birds and why?

Fig 45 . Moving scarecrow

In this example, movement is achieved by having pinwheels as hands.

Fig 46. Pakenham Mill, Suffolk, in the early 20th century.

Fig 47 . A bottle mill

These simple wind turbines made from 1pt plastic milk bottles spin very quickly when set up on top of a bamboo cane.

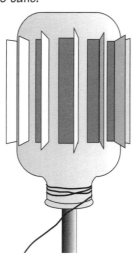

Fig 48. Wind powered generators

These two examples illustrate 'solidity' in wind generator design.

Windmills

Windmills have been used for over 2000 years. In Britain they have been common since the medieval period. By the early 19th century there were more than 10,000 windmills in Britain. They were mainly used for grinding corn, pumping water, sawing wood and making paper.

Investigate the history of wind power in your locality. Using Ordnance Survey maps of the area around the school children can look for clues of windmills in the past, for example Mill Lane, where there is no stream or river to indicate a water mill. Check out old maps of the area from the local archives office and look at old photographs or other pictures.

Bottle mills

These can be used to show the power of the wind to do work. Use a round plastic drink bottle. Cut slits in it all the way round and bend the cut parts out so that they act as sails. Up-end the bottle on a stick so that it will turn easily. Tie a piece of string around the bottle neck. Attach the other end of the string to something that can be pulled along fairly easily, such as a wheeled toy. As the wind blows the bottle round the string will wind up and the toy move. Children could try designing other work for this mill to do.

Investigating wind machines

To help children understand the principles of different wind machines let them experiment with making and using simple card or plastic wind machines which have high or low solidity. They can compare the speed in the same wind conditions, and see whether machines can turn a thread and pull a weight.

Wind machines which do mechanical work, such as traditional windmills, need a high turning force (torque) but do not need to turn fast. They have high solidity, with a large area of blade. Machines designed to generate electricity need to turn fast but do not need a high turning force (torque). In places with high wind speeds they tend to have low solidity with a few, narrow, carefully shaped blades.

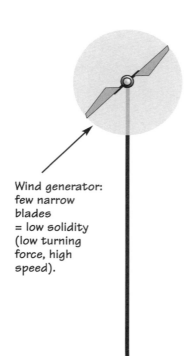

Wind generator:
few narrow
blades
= low solidity
(low turning
force, high
speed).

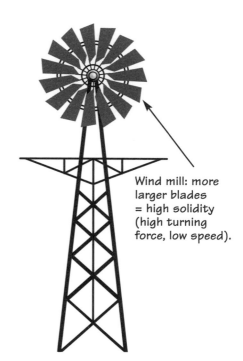

Wind mill: more
larger blades
= high solidity
(high turning
force, low speed).

Test rig for trying out different designs

Make a test rig for trying out different designs of wind machine. If you are using 'wind' from a hair dryer or air blower you will need to know the diameter of the 'blow' at a set distance from the blower. The blades should not be any bigger than the diameter of blow when testing.

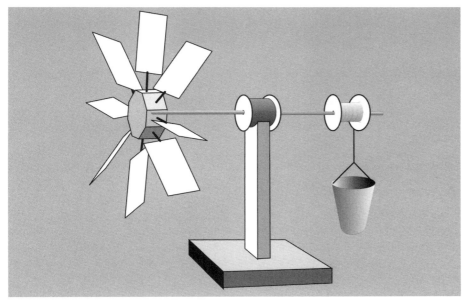

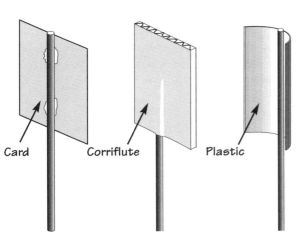

Card   Corriflute   Plastic

Propeller blade

Wooden dowel rod is probably the easiest material to use for the shaft, and a plastic cotton reel makes an excellent support for the shaft, as long as the hole is a bit bigger than the diameter of the shaft. Rub the shaft with wax to prevent friction.

Design, make and use different kinds of blades

Children should base their designs on what has been successful in the past, by looking at pictures of windmills. They need to think about the size, shape, angle, number and material of the blades or sails. They can experiment with different kinds. They also need to experiment with getting the hub and shaft right. When they are happy they have a good design, they should make a windmill. Afterwards they can evaluate the design. How could it be improved?

Fig 49. Test rig for blade designs

This can be used to measure the relative success of different blade designs. Each design is subjected to a standard wind (a desk fan that is left in the same position for each trial) and made to lift a weight in the plastic cup. The heavier the load lifted - the better the blade design.

Fig 50. Blade and hub designs

Examples of various blade and hub designs. The square batten can be drilled for push fit of dowel which in turn holds the blades, or sawn to make slots to take the blades directly. The circular hub is sawn with oblique slots to push fit the blades. The propeller blade is best obtained from a model shop.

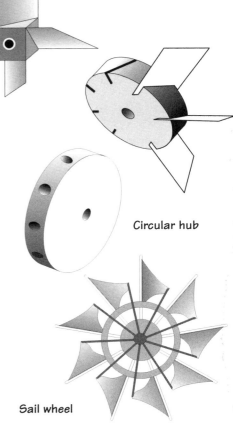

Square hub

Circular hub

Sail wheel

Model working windmill

Challenge children to make a windmill which will lift a weight. They can use what they have learnt from some of the other activities above. They can test a windmill for lifting a weight by counting the time it takes to lift a known weight up a known length of string. Older children should think about the blades, the hub, shaft and stand. Younger ones could be provided with hub, shaft and stand and concentrate on the blades only in their designs. Additional challenges might include: how can they enable the top section to move round to face into the wind? Can the working windmill be used to turn other wheels and make something turn, e.g. a model grinding stone?

Using wind to generate electricity

Windmills were first used for generating electricity at the end of the 19th century, but serious work on the engineering and technology of wind power only began in the 1970s. Today wind power is developed in Denmark, California, the Netherlands, Spain, China and India. In Britain there are now several large and many small wind farms. It may be possible to visit one near you.

Fig 51. A wind farm in Wales

Make an aerogenerator

A windmill that generates electricity is called a wind turbine or aerogenerator. Challenge the children to design, make and use an aerogenerator. They should design the blades, hub, shaft and stand and test them. Start by looking at pictures of modern aerogenerators. How are they different from traditional windmills?

To test for electricity generation you need to attach a small electric motor to the shaft. Those used for model-making will do, but are not as effective as small low friction motors (often called 'solar motors'). The shaft should be as short as possible. Most small motors have their own small shaft which can be pushed into a hole drilled in the end of your shaft. The easiest and most effective method is to use a little plastic bush as shown below right. An alternative method using a rubber or plastic tube is shown in Fig. 52.

Test the aerogenerator designs using a meter. Then you can see which designs work best and record and compare results. You can connect the motor to the meter using crocodile clips. Meters are available from Commotion (see Resources list page 63). Use one of 0-6 volts which will give you a measure of the speed of rotation.

Fig 52. Connecting the electric motor to the shaft

The diagrams show two methods of connecting the motor drive shaft to an external device.

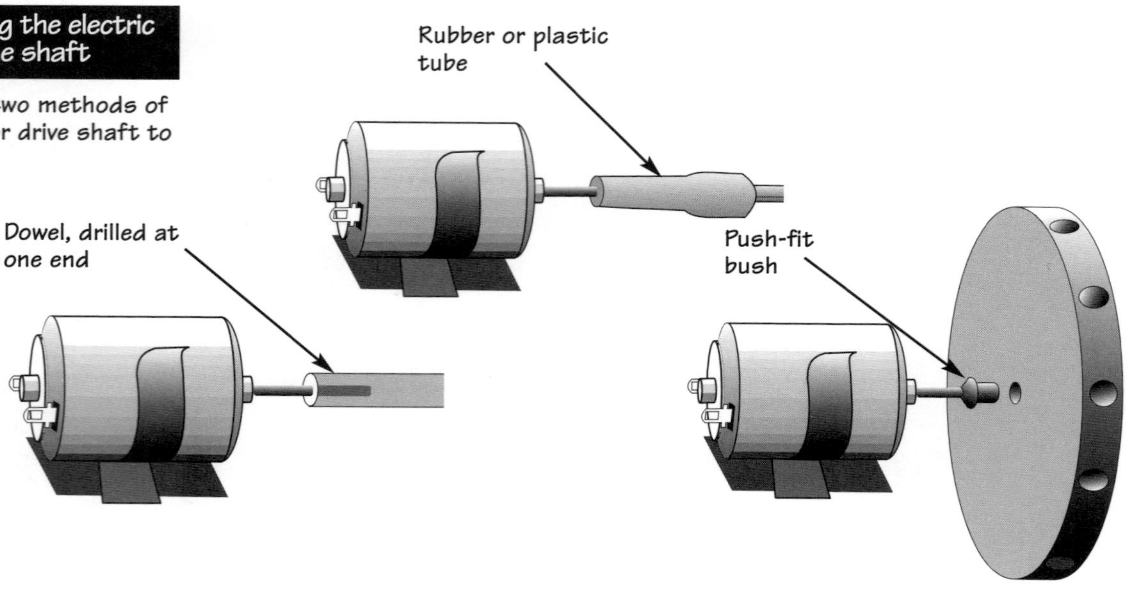

Rubber or plastic tube

Dowel, drilled at one end

Push-fit bush

Chapter 7 Storing and saving energy

How can energy be stored?

Energy is stored in plants and animals, as fossil fuels, in the form of electricity in batteries. Mechanical energy can also be stored. This can be shown easily using elastic band powered and clockwork toys, etc. Clockwork toys store mechanical energy by winding up a spring. Another good example is the recently invented clockwork radio, now being manufactured in South Africa. You might want to begin work on energy storage with activities on how plants and animals store energy (pages 20 and 26-27), and move on to consider a wide range of energy storage.

Line up a number of objects, all of which store energy, and ask children to suggest what they have in common. Include for example: a lump of coal, a small battery, a potato, an elastic band, a bottle of oil, a seed, a piece of wood. To include animal storage you could include an egg or a carton of milk, or even a snail. Discuss what form of energy each object represents, e.g. fossil fuel, food, electricity, plant or animal. Most will fall into more than one category. Discuss which are renewable and which non-renewable.

Elastic band powered boats

Make a boat powered by elastic band. The elastic band stores the mechanical energy produced when the band is turned by hand. Two different designs are shown below, but your pupils may be able to think of others.

Fig 53. Elastic band powered boats

The paddle boat (below left) requires a slot cut into one end of a small piece of timber (150mm x 75mm x 12mm is ideal). Older children may be able to cut the slot by drilling the corner points with a pillar drill, and cutting with tenon and coping saws. Let them experiment with different sizes of paddle.

The propeller driven boat (below right) requires more care in construction but no benchwork. Screw a small eye hook into the underside of the hull about 5mm from the middle of the back edge. Screw an open hook near the front as shown. Glue a stiff wire into the plastic propeller and thread one or two wood or plastic beads onto the back end behind the prop. Form a hook on the end of the wire behind the beads and thread this through the eyehook. Attach the rubber band as shown.

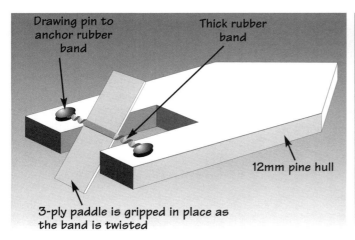

Drawing pin to anchor rubber band

Thick rubber band

12mm pine hull

3-ply paddle is gripped in place as the band is twisted

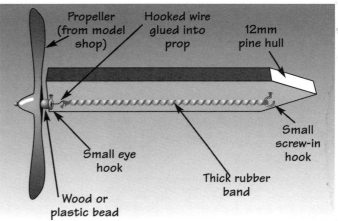

Propeller (from model shop)

Hooked wire glued into prop

12mm pine hull

Small eye hook

Wood or plastic bead

Thick rubber band

Small screw-in hook

Using energy efficiently

We can use energy more efficiently in several different ways. The aims are:

▶ to reduce the use of fossil fuels, which are non-renewable, to save some for future generations.

▶ to reduce burning of fuels such as fossil fuels, and even renewable fuels such as wood, because the gases given off pollute the atmosphere and contribute to global warming.

▶ to use energy efficiently so that it is not wasted. For example to use less energy to heat our homes by insulating them well.

▶ to save money by using less energy in our homes and schools.

To work out the saving of a CFL over an ordinary bulb:

Example:
CFL uses 20W, costs £10 and lasts 5000 hours.

Ordinary bulb uses 100W costs 50p and lasts 750 hours.

Saving over lifetime of CFL is 80 watts (100-20), times the number of hours (5000), times the price of electricity, say 10p per kWh. This works out as £40. Add to that the saving of not buying another 7 ordinary bulbs at 50p, which is £3.50. The saving is therefore £43.50.

Clockwork clocks and toys

Bring into class different kinds of clocks and watches and let the children look at how they are powered and how some use stored energy. Discuss the advantages and disadvantages of each. For example, they could compare a clockwork alarm, battery clock or watch, solar-powered watch, and sundial (see page 8).

If possible bring into class one or more clockwork toys. Compare the action of clockwork toys with battery-operated ones. What are the advantages and disadvantages?

Batteries

Let children compare the cost and length of use of batteries. Ask them to devise a fair test to compare long-life and ordinary batteries. Compare battery power with other ways of powering things. For example it may be possible to compare the cost of battery power for a radio with mains electricity. Can you compare battery power with any other types of power, for example by using some of the experiments in previous chapters? Disposing of old batteries is a problem. They contain very polluting chemicals (even nickel cadmium rechargeables) and should not go in landfill.

Comparing light bulbs

Replacing incandescent light bulbs with modern energy-efficient light bulbs is a good way to save energy and cut pollution. In the old type of light bulbs most of us use, only 10% of the energy used is converted to light. The rest is wasted as heat. Children can feel this heat given off by putting their hands near, but not too near, to such a light bulb. Compact fluorescent lamps (CFLs) are four to five times more efficient than ordinary bulbs. They last eight times longer and use only 75-80% of the electricity used by ordinary bulbs. Let children compare the energy labelling on the packaging for an ordinary bulb and a CFL. It should show energy efficiency (A to E rated), light output (lumens), power consumption (watts) and the life of the bulb in hours. If you know the price of each kind of bulb the pupils can work out which is the cheapest per hour. If children put their hands near to a CFL they can feel that it is producing less heat.

Pupils could go on to decide whether CFLs should be fitted at school, and, if so, which light fittings should get them first. Those who are good at mathematics or keen to save money could work out the potential savings at home too.

Personal energy audit

Ask children to list the activities they do through the day in half-hour slots. Then for each activity, they should think about: does it use energy of any kind? If so, what kind? For how much of any 24 hour period are they consuming energy? For what percentage of the day are they consuming fossil fuels in some way?

For example: an activity such as swimming uses their own food energy, also the energy (probably fossil fuels) to heat the swimming pool and pump the water round. How did they get to the swimming pool? An activity such as eating consumes food energy and also energy used in cooking, or perhaps in packaging or processing food, as well as transporting food, harvesting, producing fertilisers, etc.

Comparing different materials - for energy absorption and insulation

Some surfaces absorb energy and others reflect it. Some materials store energy and others pass it on. Materials which are good insulators slow down the passage of energy (heat, electricity or sound). Insulators do not store heat, they do not let it through. Materials which are good conductors pass it on more quickly.

Ask children to investigate which surfaces reflect and which absorb energy. (See also activities on solar collection in Chapter 2.) They could do this by wrapping jam jars with a variety of materials and filling them with water. Place the jam jars on a sunny window sill and measure the temperature of the water in all of them at intervals. They could try silver foil, white paper, black paper, other colours, shiny surfaces and matt surfaces. Graphs can be used to present the results.

Ask the children to investigate which materials insulate and which conduct heat well. Insulating materials bounce the heat back off them. Use a series of aluminium cans or plastic pots. Cover each one with a different material. They could try wool, paper, aluminium foil, cling film, polystyrene, cardboard. Think about the thickness of the materials. Fill each container with hot (but not boiling) water and measure the temperature of the water. Leave them all in the same place. Then measure the temperature of the water at intervals and record the results. Which container keeps the water hottest for longest?

For a real life use of this, compare the materials of cups used for serving hot drinks - china, polystyrene, cardboard, plastic. Collect a variety of different drinks cups. Devise a fair test and try it out. Can you allow for the different thicknesses of the materials? Which keeps the drink hottest?

Insulating a person

Discuss the kinds of clothes we wear in cold weather. Brainstorm the types of different clothing and list the clothes on the board. You could work from the bottom up or the top down! Then discuss the materials best suited for wear in cold weather - wool, down, fur, etc. and their synthetic alternatives. Discuss the need for different layers which trap the air, which is more effective than one thick coat. You might bring in some ski-wear, thermal underwear, or outdoor clothes catalogues for the children to look at too, or show a clip from a video of explorers/scientists in the Arctic or Antarctic. Then ask children to use the photocopiable sheet on page 58 and draw on the layers of clothes to be worn by their Arctic explorer. To get round the problem of the need for different layers, they could draw the underwear on the left, the next layer in the middle and the third layer on the right, and use labels to make the different layers and materials clear.

Go on from this to research and discuss animals' insulation and energy conservation.

Design a warm bedroom

Ask pupils to draw a plan of their own bedroom at home. They could do this on squared paper for homework. Younger children can do this as a sketch, older ones can measure and draw to scale. They should draw on it the source of heat. In most cases this will be a radiator. Is their bedroom generally too warm, just right, or not warm enough? They cannot move the radiator, but there may be ways they could make the room warmer or save on the energy used. Ask them to think about:

▶ Where is the source of heat (radiator)?

▶ Where is the heat from the radiator going? (It goes in all directions from the radiator. Warm air expands and rises. Cold air sinks and moves in to replace warm air. In this way air circulates in the room.)

▶ Are there any draughts?

▶ Is the window double-glazed?

▶ How thick are the curtains? Do they cover the window well?

▶ Do the curtains cover the radiator?

▶ Is there anything between the radiator and your bed?

▶ Has the radiator got a thermostat?

Could each pupil list three ideas to improve the warmth of their room or save energy in it?

Make model houses

Most houses lose heat in the same ways. See Fig 54 on the left.

Begin by drawing a house on the board and asking pupils to suggest how heat is lost. Then add the percentages. Ask them how we can slow down heat loss. They should suggest insulating, perhaps double-glazing and also draught proofing.

To investigate this they could, in groups, build two identical houses using cardboard boxes. Alternatively you could build one house for the class, test it uninsulated first, and then add insulation and test it again. Make a simple box-shape (you do not need rooms) and a roof which can be removed easily. It should be big enough to hold a light bulb and a thermometer. Cut and fold a door, so that it opens and closes. Cut out windows and cover with clingfilm or other clear plastic. Make sure there are no large holes in floor, walls, etc. To heat your house use an electric light bulb on a stand. You will have to cut a hole in the side of the box for the light flex. Run the light for a set period of time, with the roof on, and measure the temperature inside with a thermometer. Then turn off the light bulb, and test again for temperature at set intervals. How long does it take for the 'house' to lose its heat and go back to the same temperature as outside the box?

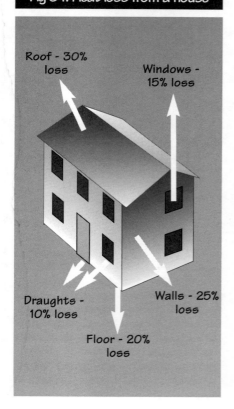

Fig 54. Heat loss from a house

Roof - 30% loss

Windows - 15% loss

Draughts - 10% loss

Walls - 25% loss

Floor - 20% loss

Make an insulated house. The pupils should suggest what materials to use to insulate the house. Materials which have little air bubbles are good insulators. The pupils will have to be careful that there is enough space left inside to hold the light bulb and not to have a fire hazard. The heat must not melt the insulation or the cling film. They should take care to insulate the roof, the floor, the walls, and the door and windows. But the door must still open and it must be possible to see through the windows. Materials such as newspaper, clingfilm, polystyrene and cardboard can all be used. The important factor is the air trapped in the insulation. Do not use fibre glass as this can give off irritating fibres. The pupils might even be able to create false inside walls or floors. Ask them to think about devising a fair test and the thickness of the different materials.

Test the insulated house in exactly the same way as the uninsulated one. Record the results. Or you could try adding one aspect of the insulation at a time: walls, then floor, then roof, etc. and see which one makes the most difference.

Discuss with the pupils what they can learn from this for insulating their own houses.

Haybox cooking

Hayboxes are insulated boxes for slow cooking. They enable you to cook a variety of foods and save energy and money. Pupils can make their own haybox cookers in groups. They will need a cardboard box or similar container, insulating material and a pot for the food.

The pupils may like to experiment with different kinds of insulation. Originally hay was used, but polystyrene and crumpled newspaper are good. It is best to make the box to fit a particular pot, as the less air around the sides of the pot the better. The cooking pot must have a well-fitting lid and handles at the top so that it can be taken out easily.

To use a haybox you will need to bring the contents of the pot to the boil on an ordinary stove or in a microwave first. Then put the pot in the haybox and close the lid of the haybox quickly. Haybox cooking is good for soups, stews, brown rice and other dishes which need slow cooking. You will need to experiment with cooking times, but do not remove the pot too often. Each time you remove it for testing or stirring you should bring the pot to the boil again on a stove before putting it back in the haybox. Approximate cooking times are: stews 3-5 hours, lentils 1-3 hours, milk puddings 1 hour. Rice pudding is a good recipe for haybox cooking.

Energy map of school

You will need some outline maps of the school grounds and buildings, including plans of the rooms. Divide the class into groups. Each group can tackle one area, such as the kitchens, the grounds, the classroom, etc. Before you begin agree on a key to show the types of energy users. Then each group should mark on a map the energy users in their area: electric sockets, lights, radiators and hot taps. Note any hot or cold spots. Why are some rooms warmer than others?

Once energy usage is mapped, then discuss the different types of energy used by different appliances. For example does the school have a gas or oil fired

Take care there is enough space around the light bulb.

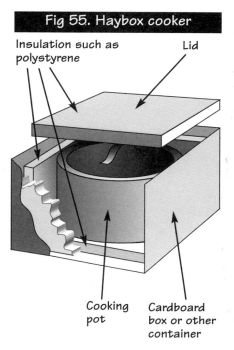

Fig 55. Haybox cooker

Insulation such as polystyrene

Lid

Cooking pot

Cardboard box or other container

Saving energy at home and school

1. Use draught-proofing and insulation.

2. Turn down heating and wear an extra jumper.

3. Close doors and windows when the heating is on.

4. Close curtains at night.

5. Turn off lights when you are not in the room.

6. Turn off appliances, and standbys including video recorders and TVs.

7. Use energy-saving appliances such as energy-saving light bulbs.

8. Fit double-glazing when you need new windows.

central heating system, and use mains electricity for office equipment? Look at the bills for the different fuels and notice how much more energy is consumed by heating than any other use. Discuss which uses are most likely to be consuming fossil fuels. Each group should then think of ways of reducing energy consumption in the area they mapped.

You could go on from this to make an energy conservation plan for the whole school with the agreement of the headteacher, other teachers, parents, governors, the caretaker. Or you could ask children to make signs for their own classroom to encourage good energy use, or adapt this idea for their homes.

Conserving energy in school

Once children have completed a map of school energy use or an energy audit, ask them to consider ways energy could be saved without compromising safety. This could include inventive drawn or junk modelled designs for replacing old 'terrapin' or other outdoor classrooms with purpose-built energy-saving rooms. County architects may have information to help with with energy-efficient school designs. Alternatively pupils could design posters asking other children and staff to conserve energy, or consult kitchen and other staff to see whether there are potential savings in kitchens, hot water systems, heating and lighting. Would going home earlier in winter (compensated for by longer hours in summer!) help to save energy?

Draughtometer

Tape a piece of soft toilet tissue to a pencil or pen so that the tissue hangs loose. Blow on it to see how much 'blow' is needed to make it move. Use the draughtometer to test at school or home to find draughts around doors, windows and other places.

Home appliances

Ask children, for homework, to make a list of all the appliances or machines at home which use energy of some sort. They could also draw them. They can then (at home, or back in school) say what kind of power each uses.

From this it is possible for each child to make their own mapping diagram for energy sources. List the appliances down one side of the page, and the types of power down the other side. They should then connect each appliance to the correct source of power with a line. A photocopiable sheet for this activity is provided on page 60.

Investigating meters at home

Ask children to look at their electricity meter at home. They should look at it at different times and count how many units are being used in half an hour:

▶ when no appliances are being used (apart from fridge/freezer and anything else which is left on all the time);

▶ when only one light bulb is on;

▶ when one large appliance is on (e.g. iron, washing machine, oven);

▶ at a very busy period, when several different appliances are being used.

What do they notice about the number of units being used?

Life without electricity

If you are studying Victorian Britain, this provides a good opportunity to see what other sources of power people used. Look at photos and old artefacts, such as flat irons. Parents may have appropriate 'antiques' so that you could make a class museum of these. Or you could invite someone from a local museum to bring in artefacts. Even in Britain in the early 20th century many people lived without electricity. Some children may know older people who remember when electricity was a luxury. Invite them into class to be interviewed.

What would you do in the evening with no electricity?

Begin by asking the class what activities they do in the evening at home. Make a list on the board and then ask them to tell you which ones use electricity. Which activities are left? What other things could they do which would not need electricity? Compare summer and winter. What did people do in the past?

This is an Arctic explorer.

Draw on the layers of clothes he or she would need to wear. Label the clothes and materials used.

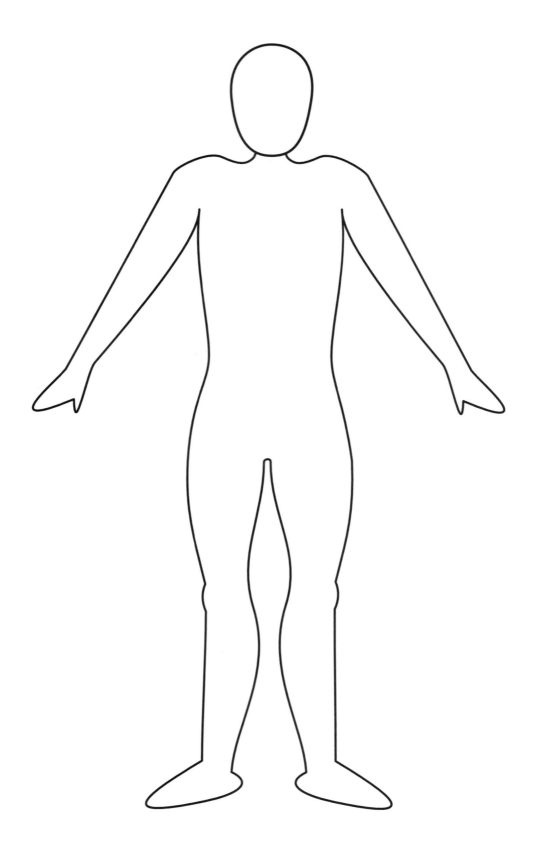

Home Energy Saving

Use what you have learnt about energy saving to survey your own home. Look around your home very carefully and talk to your parent or guardian.

Give your home a score of between 0 and 10 for each point. 0 if nothing has been done, 10 if everything possible has been done.

SCORE

Lighting

▶ 1. Modern energy efficient light bulbs? ---

▶ 2. Always switch off lights when no one in the room. -------------------------------

Heating

▶ 3. Radiators have thermostatic controls? ---

▶ 4. Temperature is cool enough to need a jumper when heating is on. ----------------------

Hot water

▶ 5. Hot water pipes are lagged (insulated).--

▶ 6. Hot water tank has a thick jacket. --

Cooking

▶ 7. Use microwave rather than large oven. ---

▶ 8. Use gas rather than other fuels (more efficient).---------------------------------

Electrical equipment

▶ 9. Modern, efficient equipment?---

▶ 10.TV, video, etc switched off when not in use: not left on standby. ------------------------

Insulation

▶ 11. Windows and doors are closed when heating is on?---------------------------------

▶ 12. Windows are double glazed?--

▶ 13. Doors and windows have draught proofing?--

▶ 14. Roof space insulated?---

▶ 15. Curtains are thick and drawn at night? --

The maximum score is 150. If your home scores over 100 you are doing well.

Some of the things in the list above cost nothing. Mark those with an asterisk. Others can be quite costly. Is there anything else which could be done at little or no cost?

total

Energy sources and stores

The list on the left shows some sources and stores of energy you may have in your home. On the right make a list of the different things in your home which use energy. Then connect each thing to the correct source of energy by drawing a line. Do not forget to include things such as calculators, door bells and personal stereos.

Energy sources and stores

Things which use energy to work

mains electricity

gas

oil

coal

wood

battery

solar panel

_____

_____

_____

_____

_____

_____

_____

_____

_____

_____

_____

_____

_____

Links between the activities and the Programmes of Study in the National Curriculum for England and Wales and the National Guidelines in Scotland for Environmental Studies.

(References refer to KS2 only though many activities are also suitable for KS1 or KS3. Experimental and Investigative Science has not been included because it is addressed by most activities.)

Activity	NC links England and Wales	Scotland
The sun in the solar system	Sc Phys Proc 3,4. Maths U & A	2, 3
Shadow clock	Sc Phys Proc 3	2,3
Measuring shadows	Geog 8, D&T, Sc Phys Proc 3	2,3
Sundials	Geog 8, D&T, Sc Phys Proc 3,4	3
Observing cloud cover	Geog 8, Maths U & A	4
Sunshine plan of school grounds	Geog 8,3. Sc Phys Proc 3,4. Maths U & A	4
Sun drying	Sc Mat 2, Geog 8	
Evaporation	Sc Mat 2, Geog 8	
Heat-storing greenhouse	Sc Mat 1, Phys Proc 3, D&T, Geog 10b, Maths U & A	
Collecting solar energy	Sc Mat 2, Phys Proc 3	2
Using colours to absorb and reflect the sun's energy	Sc Mat 1,2	2,3
Using different materials to absorb or reflect the sun's energy	Sc Mat 1,2. Phys Proc 3,	2,3
Solar cooking	Sc Mat 2, D&T	2,3
A solar oven	Sc Mat 2, D&T	2,3
Apple baking	Sc Mat 2, D&T	2,3
Parabola cooker	Sc Mat 2, Phys Proc 3	2,3
Passive solar heating	Sc Phys Proc 3	2
Hot water heater	Sc Mat 2 D&T	3
Using photovoltaic cells	Sc Phys Proc 1,3	2
Plants as solar collectors	Sc Life Proc 1,3	1
Map of solar collectors	Geog 8, 3 Sc Life Proc 1,3	2
Plants store energy	Sc Life Proc 1,3	1
Beans in a jar	Sc Life Proc 1,3,5, Maths U & A	1
Investigating trees' leaves	Sc Life Proc 3,5, Maths U & A	1
Lengths of growing seasons and day-length	Geog 8, Sc Life Proc 5	2,1
Plants move towards the sun	Sc Life Proc 3,5	1
Plants as food/Energy chains	Sc Life Proc 1,2,5	1
Composting	Sc Life Proc1,5, Mat 2	1
Fossil fuel audit	Geog 10, Sc Mat 2	2
Bonfires	Sc Mat 2	
Charcoal burning clamp	Sc Mat 2, Hist 5, 3a/b	5
Locality studies	Geog 4/5	
Plant oils	Sc Mat 1,2. Hist 1,3a. Geog 4/5	2,5
Alternative plant fuels	Geog 10,4/5	2
Food chains for plants and animals paper chains	Sc Life Proc 1,5	1
Energy chains in the school grounds	Sc Life Proc 1,5	1
Growth monitoring of small animals	Maths U & A, Sc Life Proc 5	1
How much do animals eat?	Maths U & A, Sc Life Proc 5	1
Working animals	Sc Life Proc 5, Geog 4/5. Hist 2, 3a	5
Food kilometres	Geog 10, Maths U & A	6
Energy labels on food packets	D&T, Sc Life Proc 2	6
High energy drinks	D&T, Sc Life Proc 2	2
Energy for a school meal	Sc Life Proc1,2, Geog 10	
Our own energy	Sc Life Proc 2	1
Self-energy audit/diary	Sc Life Proc 2	
Human power	Sc Life Proc 2	
Clockwork and elastic band power	D&T, Sc Phys Proc 2	
Bicycles and gears	D&T, Sc Phys Proc 2	
A model of the water cycle	Geog 7, 8.	3
Experimenting with water pressure	Sc Phys Proc 2, D&T	

Activity	NC links England & Wales	Scotland
A model water-powered turbine	D&T, Sc Phys Proc 2	2,3,4
A simple turbine	D&T, Sc Phys Proc 2	2,3
Water wheels in history	D&T, Hist 1,2,3a,3b,5	3,4,5
Make an overshot wheel	D&T, Sc Phys Proc 2	3,4
Make an undershot wheel	D&T, Sc Phys Proc 2	3,4
Investigate water power designs	D&T, Sc Phys Proc 1	3
Water power in your environment	Geog 7,9,10	3,4
Measuring stream flow	Maths U & A, Sc Phys Proc 2	
Measuring the head	Maths U & A, Sc Phys Proc 2	
Using the senses	Geog 8, Sc Liv Proc 2	3,4
Weather watch	Geog 8	3,4
The wet finger test	Geog 8	3,4
Wind socks	Geog 8, D&T	3,4
Weather vanes	Geog 8, D&T	3,4
Wind roses	Geog 8, Maths U & A	3,4
Wind speed	Geog 8, D&T	3,4
Pinwheels	D&T, Sc Phys Proc 2	
Cup spinners	D&T, Sc Phys Proc 2	
Cloth strips	D&T, Sc Phys Proc 2	4
Wind gauges or anemometers	Geog 8, Maths U & A	3,4
Wind map of school grounds	Geog 3,8,10	3,4
Litter and leaves	Geog 10	
Kites	D&T, Sc Phys Proc 2	
Yachts	D&T, Sc Phys Proc 2	
History of sailing ships	Hist 2,3a	5
Moving scarecrows	D&T	
Windmills	D&T, Geog 4,10 Hist 2,3a/b,	
Bottle mills	D&T	
Investigating wind machines	D&T, Sc Phys Proc 1	2
Design, make and use different kinds of blades	D&T, Sc Phys Proc 2	
Model working windmill	D&T	
Using wind to generate electricity	D&T, Geog 8, Sc Phys Proc 1	2
Make an aerogenerator	D&T, Sc Phys Proc 1	2
Elastic band powered boats	D&T, Sc Phys Proc 2	
Clockwork clocks and toys	D&T, Hist 3a/b	
Batteries	Sc Phys Proc 1, Maths U & A	2
Comparing light bulbs	Sc Phys Proc 1,3, Maths U & A	2
Personal energy audit	Maths U & A, Sc Life Proc 2	
Comparing different materials - for energy absorption and insulation	Sc Mat 1,2	3
Insulating a person	Sc Mat 1, Geog 8, Sc Life Proc 1	1
Design a warm bedroom	D&T, Sc Mat 1	6
Make model houses	D&T, Geog 8	6
Haybox cooking	D&T, Sc Mat 2	3
Energy map of school	Geog 3,8. D&T	4
Conserving energy in school	Geog 10, D&T	2,6
Draughtometer	D&T	
Home appliances	Sc Phys Proc 1, D&T	2,6
Investigating meters at home	Maths U & A, Sc Phys Proc 1	2,6
Life without electricity	Hist 3a	2,6
What would you do in the evening with no electricity?	D&T	2

Key for Scottish Guidelines:

Science	Social
Understanding Living Things 1	Understanding People and Places 4
Understanding Energy and Forces 2	Understanding People in the Past 5
Understanding Earth and Space 3	Understanding People in Society 6

Technology requirements are addressed by the same activities as those marked D&T for the English curriculum.

Resources

▶ Equipment and Suppliers

1. **An automatic weather station**, 'Weather Reporter', which continuously records wind speed and direction, temperature, hours of sunshine and daylight, rainfall, pressure and humidity, is available from: The Advisory Unit, Computers in Education, 126 Great North Road, Hatfield, Herts AL9 5JZ.

2. **Equipment for measuring and recording on computer**, light, temperature and pressure is available from: Commotion Ltd., Unit 11, Tannery Rd, Tonbridge, Kent;
Data Harvest Educational Electronics, Woburn Lodge, Waterloo Rd., Linslade, Leighton Buzzard, Beds. LU7 7NR;
Philip Harris Education, Lynn Lane, Shenstone, Lichfield, Staffs, WS14 OEE

3. **Potato powered clock** is available from Intermediate Technology, 103-105, Southampton Row, London WC1B 4HH. Also clockwork radio, solar shower, low-energy lights, plugs, etc.

4. **Solar observatory**, solar system poster kit, orbit orrery, planet orrery and orbit tellerium are available from: Commotion Ltd., Unit 11, Tannery Rd, Tonbridge, Kent.
Also a voltmeter.

5. **Make a sundial book**, shadow stick and related materials, also hubs with holes, available from Technology Teaching Systems, Freephone 0800 318686, freefax 0800 137525.

6. **Solar kits,** a hand-held anemometer, small motors, clockwork/solar radios, and a range of publications are available from C.A.T.

▶ Organisations

Association for Science Education
College Lane,
Hatfield, AL10 9AA

Centre for Alternative Technology
Machynlleth, Powys, SY20 9AZ

Centre for Sustainable Energy
B-Bond Warehouse,
Smeaton Rd,
Bristol, BS1 6XN

Council for Environmental Education
94, London Street,
Reading,
Berkshire, RG1 4SJ

CREATE (Centre for Research, Education & Training in Energy)
Kenley House,
25, Bridgeman Terrace,
Wigan, WN1 1SY

Eco-Schools - run by the Tidy Britain Group
Tidy Britain Group,
The Pier,
Wigan,
Lancs, WN3 4EX

Energy Saving Trust
11-12, Buckingham Gate,
London, SW1E 6LB

Geographical Association
160, Solly Street,
Sheffield, S1 4BF

Global Action Plan
8 Fulwood Place,
London, WC1V 6HG

Going for Green
Elizabeth House,
The Pier,
Wigan, WN3 4EX

Groundwork (Young Energy Savers)
85, Cornwall Street,
Birmingham, B3 3BY

Henry Doubleday Research Association
National Centre for Organic Gardening,
Ryton on Dunsmore,
Coventry, CV 8 3LG

Learning through Landscapes
Third Floor, Southside Offices,
The Law Courts,
Winchester,
Hampshire, SO23 9DL

National Spring Clean run by the Tidy Britain Group (see above)

Powersavers
Centrica plc,
Charter Court,
50, Windsor Road,
Slough, SL1 2HA

Schoolenergy - (previously Energy Cashback) run by CREATE

The Sunpower Club
Freepost No PT 669,
127, Bath Rd,
Southsea, PO4 OHX

Wasting Energy Costs the Earth
PO Box 200,
Stratford upon Avon,
Warwickshire, CV 37 9ZZ

World Wide Fund for Nature
Panda House, Weyside Park,
Godalming,
Surrey, GU7 1XR

**Young Energy Savers is run by
Groundwork (Head Office)**
85, Cornwall Street,
Birmingham, B3 3BY

 References

Geography in the School Grounds,
Hare, Attenborough and Day, Southgate/LTL

Make a Sundial
British Sundial Society

Science in the School Grounds, Thomas
LTL/Southgate

**Understanding Global Issues:
Renewable Energy**, European
Schoolbooks Publishing Ltd, The Runnings,
Cheltenham, GL51 9QR

Energy Watch
Newsletter from CREATE

C.A.T. Publications
Teacher's Guides to Renewable Energy
Projects - Windpower
Teacher's Guides to Renewable Energy
Projects - Solar Heating
Pupil's Guide to Windpower (written for
KS4+)
Pupil's Guide to Solar Power (written for
KS4+)
Activities for Children (KS2)